A Kid Just Like Me

A Kid Just Like Me

A Father and Son Overcome the Challenges
of ADD and Learning Disabilities

Bruce Roseman, M.D.

A Perigee Book

A Perigee Book
Published by The Berkley Publishing Group
A division of Penguin Putnam Inc.
375 Hudson Street
New York, New York 10014

Copyright © 2001 by Bruce Roseman, M.D.
Text design by Tiffany Kukec
Cover design by Royce M. Becker
Cover photo courtesy of Ellen Roseman

First edition: September 2001
Published simultaneously in Canada.

Visit our website at
www.penguinputnam.com

Library of Congress Cataloging-in-Publication Data

Roseman, Bruce.
    A kid just like me: a father and son overcome the challenges of ADD
and learning disabilities / Bruce Roseman.
        p.   cm.
    Includes index.
    ISBN 0-399-52686-2
    1. Roseman, Bruce—Mental health.   2. Roseman, Joshua—Mental
health.   3. Attention-deficit hyperactivity disorder—Patients—
Biography.   4. Attention-deficit-disordered children—Biography.
5. Learning disabilities—Biography.   I. Title.
RJ506.H9 R665   2001
618.92'8589'0092—dc21
    [B]   00-050200

Printed in the United States of America

10   9   8   7   6   5   4   3   2   1

dedication

To Larry Lynn,
Because he has always treated me with respect,
And it has always mattered.

Contents

acknowledgments

I am thankful to the many patients and friends who have provided me with the inspiration, guidance and courage to continue.

Marcia Amsterdam: My book guru. The thousands of times I excitedly called at odd hours, just to hear "there, there, there," after which I would heave a sigh of relief and lapse into tranquillity. I cannot imagine writing a book without a person like this to explain it all to me.

Steve and Alex Cohen for their decency, charity of spirit, moral, and financial support. They stepped up to the plate in the bottom of the ninth, with two outs, the count 0 and 2 and smacked a home run, and made the rest of the team believe that the game could be won.

Jerry Gross provided editorial help, sage advice, and

cheerleading. He taught me how to write without telling me what to write. It is one of the most generous gifts I have ever received from another human being.

Denise and Al Hurley, whose efforts on behalf of me, Joshua, and Gateway, bring me to tears every single time I think about it, which I do often.

Patricia Herbich, the initial spark. Uncharacteristically I kept Pat waiting in my office on a busy day. She happened to glance down at my characteristically cluttered floor and saw some of my scribblings on the floor next to her chair. Instead of complaining about the long wait she said, "Is it okay if I read this?" then "Let me help you with this," then "Could I show it to David Vigliano?" I said, "Who is David Vigliano?"

Mark and Anla Cheng Kingdon, for their longstanding and ongoing support.

Larry Lynn—my friend for forty-five years, encouraged, cajoled, corrected, suggested, and believed.

Dr. Dina Mendes for telling me "You have to take care of your own child. No one else can or will."

Deborah November, an editor and friend of my wife and family, who was kind enough to read through my original manuscript and give me credibility with my family and myself.

Ken Plevin, for carrying Gateway on his back for as long as it took to save it, and for being the consummate role model for any parent with a special needs child. To his son Jeffrey for being a shining example of how well things can work out.

Sheila Curry Oakes, my editor at Penguin—she understood me, what I was trying to say, and did a masterful job bringing both to the printed page.

LeAnn Rimes, whose angelic pure voice came to me through my headphones, inspiring me to write and allowing me to focus as I listened to her albums over and over and over and over.

Kenneth Rosenberg, M.D.: psychiatrist and filmmaker, who provided insightful advice and encouragement at our weekly pizza meetings to discuss the progress of the book.

Carolyn Salzman, for letting me see how helping a child can light up ones life.

Naomi Thornton for explaining to me that women want to know and understand "their sons and fathers and brothers."

David Vigliano, my agent. This book is a direct result of his vision, direction, and faith. I could never have done this without him.

Ellen Wahl, for being my longest-standing patient and supporter and telling me about the Flying Dolphins.

Linda Watrous, who became a sounding board every week when she came in for an allergy shot. As an educator she told me that I had something to say, inspired me to say it, and critiqued it after I said it. She told me about the Gateway school, and there are not enough thanks in the world for that.

My wife, Ellen, who reads to me because I cannot, keeps me calm, and has put up with my quirks, quests, obsessions, and adventures for almost twenty years while giving me two sweet wonderful children.

Aaron: my son, for being so undisturbed by it all, taking care of me when I got sick, accepting his brother without judging him, and for letting me see the other side.

My father, who taught me about the responsibility to right the wrongs.

My mother, who never understood, but always found the strength to support me in whatever I did.

My grandpa Harry and grandma Frieda, for loving me unconditionally.

Elyssa Barbaro, Jennifer Bush, Loretta Cuoco, for having the strength and decency to cry over my book; Diane Mancher; Mandie DeVincentes; The Flying Dolphins Swim Team of The 92nd Street Y and their coach, Cesar; everyone at the Gateway School; Donna Gould; Phil Hanrahan; Amy Karp; Kevin Saer; Judith Searle; Andrea Schulz; Lisa Sharkey; Richard Smith; Tony Villella; Lucy Wheeler; my patients, who stuck with me through the hard times and cared; my college physics teacher; and finally, Peter Mott, may he rest in peace, and his wife, Wanla Cheng, who always took time from their problems to ask how Joshua and I were doing, and offer encouragement.

Thank you all. If I forgot to name anyone please understand that I will always remember you in my heart.

Love,
Bruce Roseman

This book is topical; it is a story for and of our times. The educational system in this country is under attack for stilted teaching methods and dismal outcomes. The number of children classified as "Learning Disabled" is staggering, estimated at ten to twenty percent of the school population. The number of adults with these problems is inestimable.

The professional and lay literature is rife with articles on Attention Deficit Disorder (ADD/ADHD) Word Retrieval, Sequencing, and Dyslexia, yet the treatment of these learning "problems" is far from satisfactory. The afflicted suffer a well documented and startling incidence of substance abuse, crime, and dysfunctional family and work lives.

Joshua and I overcame enormous obstacles because we shared an intense love for each other, burning determination, fearlessness in the face of an indifferent and hostile bureaucracy, the financial and intellectual resources to wage a war, and luck.

It is my hope that others will read this book and be inspired or educated and that they or their loved ones will be spared the heartache, shame, and sadness I have known and from which I rescued my son.

introduction

This book is about my son and myself.

It is about a learning disabled father erasing a lifetime of shame and humiliation by teaching his learning disabled son to read.

It is about a learning disabled child healing his father's wounds.

It is about vilification, vindication, and redemption.

It is about love.

I taught my son Joshua to read. On my part, it was a staggering commitment in scope and effort. On Joshua's part it was much more.

Like my son Joshua, I was perfectly happy until the age of five. It was then, as my mother has often remarked, that school robbed me of my happiness. My twin afflictions—Learning Disabilities and Attention Deficit Disorder—were unheard of in those days. I was simply a kid who was considered "unteachable" by teachers, "unreachable" by child psychologists, and "unbearable" to my own family. My mother's anguished refrain, *"I hope you have one just like you and then you will understand,"* still resonates in my mind. I knew she didn't *really* mean it. But her wish *had* come true. Joshua *was* just like me.

I always thought that if I did have a child like myself I would know what to do. I was wrong. Back in the 1950s, millions of children were demeaned, left back, and written off by teachers, psychologists, and school administrators. I was one of those children; the memories of that frustration, heartache, and shame have shaped my life. I told myself I would not allow the home I shared with my wife, Ellen, and our two young sons to be overwhelmed by stress, frustration, and despair like the home I knew growing up. I had come a long way from my painful childhood and I assumed society had come a long way, too. After all, some of my elementary school teachers had been born in the nineteenth century, and we were now heading into the twenty-first. Moreover, Attention Deficit Disorder and Learning Disabilities had been the subject of many credible medical studies. These studies had shown that up to twenty percent of school-age children exhibit some form of learning disability: a disturbing percentage, but apparently the problem was being aggressively addressed. Educational systems were beginning to employ legions of specialists to diagnose, monitor, and assist children with Attention Deficit Disorder and Learning Disabilities. Public awareness was no longer a problem. "Attention Deficit Disorder" had recently graced the cover of *Time* magazine. Trial lawyers were using Attention Deficit Disorder as a criminal defense. A child with ADD and Learning Disabilities would be able to get all the help he needed. It's amazing how sure one can be, and how wrong.

Joshua, our striking, athletic, popular child, after an auspicious beginning in school became the focal point of family turmoil. His teachers regularly battered us with a litany of "uns"—unmanageable, unteachable, and unreachable, and pointed out that, as parents, we were "in denial," "hostile," "negligent." Consultations with numerous experts and specialists forecast dismal if contradictary scenarios. Trying to deal with all of the problems caused a serious rift in my marriage and problems with my other son Aaron and left me questioning my own beliefs. Finally, in a last ditch effort to save myself, my family, and my son, I determined to teach

Joshua something that all the experts said he could not do: read.

I analyzed Joshua's problems, charting the unusual pathways in his brain, and created a map to guide me. I analyzed each strength and weakness and sought answers by drawing on my medical training as well as knowledge gleaned from a lifetime of dealing with my own disabilities. It became an extraordinary journey of both the heart and the mind. During our educational safari we would prevail over insensitive teachers, callous school administrators, the local Board of Education, and an array of self important professionals, specialists, and charlatans. We fought the good fight, standing shoulder to shoulder, and we triumphed. I taught Joshua to read by creating radical methods to address his needs, out of which came a method from which others may now benefit. I also learned something from a little boy about forgiveness, love, and acceptance.

It is *mostly* over now. The excitement of the educational safari has been replaced by Joshua's insatiable quest for knowledge. He is motivated to, and capable of, learning by himself.

Joshua is eleven years old. Any thought of him being unable to read now seems absurd. He reads milk cartons and cereal boxes by the dozen, the sports section of *The New York Times*, young reader books on history, and adult science fiction at an astonishing rate.

Naturally we understand that Joshua is *different*. He will *always* be different because of how he understands the world and how the world understands him. I cannot help studying Joshua as he interacts with the world. I watch him get confused, often without seeking clarification. He has resigned himself to the fact that he will simply not understand certain things. No one else notices, but it worries me, and it is painful to watch. Yet certain episodes in Joshua's short life have given me pause. Is it possible that the *dis* in *dis*ability may actually *dis*guise the *a* in ability?

chapter one

Joshua in the Beginning

Eight hours after saying "I do," and two hours after starting our honeymoon, Joshua was conceived. Ellen's uncharacteristic napping a few weeks later, inspired a hastily drawn blood test, which confirmed what we both already knew. We were in a state of shock, but we were thrilled.

In the womb Joshua was in perpetual motion: explosive kicking and endless squirming. I knew from experience that meant a very active child was on the way, and was soon half kidding that Joshua was going to be a hyperactive maniac just like his father. Ellen, having always been in awe of my energy level, would remark, "What's wrong with him being like his daddy?" She had a point, and momentarily, flattery would obscure the thought of, "What if this baby *is* just like me, and not like his calm, cool, and collected mother?"

Ellen went into an astonishingly fast, easy labor and Joshua was born, eyes wide open and screaming. The doctor proudly hoisted his catch, who was furiously kicking and fighting like a great fish on a hook. What fun, I thought, to behold a little baby so obviously full of life. Over the next four glorious hours I cradled this squirming bundle of energy. I marveled at how alike the newborn's movements were to the ones in utero, the ones that had caused my nervous half jokes about his hyperactivity. Within days we were drolly referring to him as "gifted," in reference to his penchant for squirming, and calling him "Squirmo."

I am a worrier and I was immediately concerned about two things. The first was that he seemed to have a small mouth. I realized that this was just the silliness of an overly critical new daddy who was also a doctor. After all, who ever suffered from a small mouth? I joked that he would just have to eat smaller sandwiches. The second thing that worried me was his high level of activity, which I told myself was just as silly as worrying about his small mouth.

Joshua was a terrific, if active, baby. He was easy to please and always in a good mood. My grandmother was always amazed at how "you could change his mind." It was true. He was always ready, willing, and able to move on to the next thing. If the milk wasn't ready yet, okay, he was just as happy to play. If he couldn't find a particular toy he would play with a different one. He never minded driving in a car or being passed around from person to person, and didn't cry when he went to the doctor and got his shots.

In the blink of an eye a personality was emerging. He was spirited, cheerful, and sweet. His explosive movements soon became more focused into lightning-fast crawling. I reveled in his sweet disposition but I worried about his quickness and energy. Ellen would often remark that I finally had something that could keep me busy: chasing after Joshua. She had a point. It was fun. He never got tired and neither did I.

I am an early riser and always have been. Each day when I awoke I would rush to Joshua's room. Invariably he would be lying in his crib, eyes open, his head pressed up against the corner of the crib, as if he were trying to push his way out. Some parental snooping coupled with my early rising soon helped me discover that Joshua lay awake in his crib for about two hours every morning before making a sound. I peeked into his room every morning, and sometimes I would just sit on the floor and watch him, endlessly fascinated by this explosive miracle of life. I had to be perfectly still because it was clear, early on, that he was exquisitely sensitive to sound. His head would pop up at the turn of the key in the front door or a footstep on the carpet. I tried to stop looking in on him because if he heard the slightest sound his head would immediately perk up and would not lie down again. He would drag himself up the side of the crib with his hands and balance himself and jump nonstop, hurling his body furiously into the railing until I picked him up. He would never cry; he would just jump with an intensity and fury that was so unsettling I would feel compelled go in and play with him. Ellen would ask, "Did you wake him up again so you could have someone to play with?" I would try to explain but it was no use. I wondered if she was right.

Ellen said I was spoiling him. She was right about that one. Pretty soon Joshua figured out that I could be manipulated in ways that Ellen could not. He came to expect me to be up in the morning, and he began looking out for me. When I tried to peek in I would see him peeking back out at me. It was okay though. We were both thankful for the company. We were the only ones up at that hour, and we were both ready for action.

One morning when Joshua was just eight months old I peeked into his room and was unnerved to not see him peeking back at me. In fact, I did not see him at all. I bolted into his room and almost tripped over him. He was crawling around on the floor. The sides of his crib were up and I realized that there was only one way he could have gotten out. He had catapulted himself out of his crib. Just eight months old, he could not stand without holding on, much less walk or climb. While in the throes of his furious jumping I had seen him try to catapult himself over the crib side, but it had never occurred to me that he could actually do it. And even if he was capable of such a thing, I would have expected him to cry when he hit the ground. But there he was lying on the floor and crawling around happily. I told Ellen when she awoke and she was incredulous until later in the week when we both saw him come flying out of his playpen.

We came to refer to his maneuver as the "great escape" and had a good laugh over it. We discussed getting a covered crib but instead got him a bed. He never fell out.

Once Joshua had mastered walking, I quickly realized that it was virtually impossible to watch him closely enough. He moved too quickly and he had absolutely no fear. He would take off without looking back and climb and run in a way that defied gravity. I finally put him in a baby harness, but it was clear to everyone that it was actually a leash. People on the street gave us disapproving looks and I felt guilty, but I simply accepted the reality that Joshua was too fast and I could not keep up with him. No one could.

At about two years of age the play dates started. When we went to someone's house we would always ask if it was baby proofed. We would get answers like, "Oh, yes, we hired professionals," or "My husband spent ten hours crawling around on his hands and knees baby proofing the place." Joshua would visit, and we came to anticipate the look of horror on the other parents' face's as they realized that baby proofing their house for their kids and baby proofing for Joshua was a horse of a very different color.

Ellen belonged to a moms group, an informal get-together for mothers and children, who met every Tuesday in the park. It was very nice, and sometimes I would attend. The kids all liked each other and played nicely together. But everyone knew about Joshua. You had to keep your eyes on him every second, or you would find him climbing a tree or the rocks or doing things that were dangerous that the other kids in the group would never attempt. He would run fast—really fast. Sometimes he would fall and scrape his knees or his chin and would bleed. But he would never cry. He would lay still for a moment, consider his injuries, and then as suddenly as he had fallen he would bounce back up and continue on at a frenetic pace. Despite his repertoire of dangerous activities, Joshua never really seemed to hurt himself. He had an uncanny sense of balance. This made him even bolder, and everyone eventually became comfortable with his doing more dangerous things than the other children because he was Joshua.

Joshua grew into a very striking child. In fact, he was gorgeous, with a sculpted physique that drew looks from everyone. Even at a young age the little girls were mysteriously attracted to him. Somehow he knew instinctively that he could not be rough with them. He could be very rough and tumble with the boys but with the girls he was gentle—and he always listened to them when they talked. He would play house with the girls, but in an instant he would be wrestling, jumping, climbing, throwing a ball, or doing whatever with the boys. He also became very protective of the girls in the group. He would not let any of the boys hurt them. One time he was on the other side of the playground and he saw a bigger boy push one of the girls in the group to the ground. Joshua exploded and made a direct line for the boy and jumped on him and bit his face as my wife rushed to pull him off the kid. Ellen was mortified and apologized profusely to the boy's mother and offered to pay for a doctor visit. To everyone's shock and amazement the mother said, "It was good for him. He is a bully and maybe now he has learned his lesson." And so it went for Joshua. People just did not seem to be able to get angry with him. The girls liked him, the boys liked him, and the parents liked him. He was immensely popular with parents. In fact, he did not seem to distinguish between the kids and the adults. He would just as easily interact with the parents as with the children. Everyone assumed he was precocious, but I had a sense that he was just confused.

Ellen also noticed these peculiarities about Joshua, but she did not see it as a problem. After all, the kid was gorgeous, sweet, and happy, and lived with a seductively dangerous abandon. She just assumed that other parents were not as good at baby proofing their houses as we were, or that that he had a fearless nature that would stand him in good stead in life. She also figured he was just an early riser like his dad. I, however, was beginning to develop a slightly different point of view. It was being driven home every morning at 5:15 A.M. Ellen has never been a "morning person." She did not like to get up for school when she was a child, and after college she worked in the theater and fit right in because theater people wake up late and go to sleep late. It is the nature of the business. So she never actually witnessed the mania Joshua and I exhibited every morning at 5:15 when Joshua woke me up to play.

I loved waking up early for some quality time with my boy. I didn't need much sleep, anyway, and I thought of it as a form of male bonding. Ellen thought it was nice that the boys got up together and were having fun while she slept. So, at 5:15 A.M. Joshua and I awoke to do all sorts of stuff. We would run around and play games and wrestle and generally horse around. I was usually the horse, but not always. I took wonderful home movies and photographs documenting those great times and I look at them often. It was great fun and we were becoming great friends. But even then I realized that what we were doing was odd. After all, it was two hours before most other people were waking up, and our level of activity was extraordinary. But there was another odd thing that I began to notice when Joshua was between two and three years old. We made a wacky sort of sense to each other and we both knew it was more than just friendship. We understood each other in a nonverbal way, and we both thought it was great. Soon it became clear that I seemed to be the only one who could easily understand him or communicate with him. His speech was developing very slowly, and as a result I translated his nonverbal communications into words and I communicated to him what others wanted. People said the reason he was not speaking was that I spoiled him by simply anticipating his thoughts and effectively becoming his translator. It was odd but cute, and everyone just sort of shrugged and figured we would both grow out of it.

We would hit the park at around 6:30 A.M., Joshua in his stroller, me in my running gear. Joshua loved it. He loved being out in the fresh air, and looking at the sights and the other sleepy-eyed joggers. We, of course, were hardly sleepy-eyed; we had been wrestling for the past hour. I was beginning realize something about Joshua's level of activity: it was impossible to tire him out.

I wondered about the possibility of a learning disorder based on all the discussion in the medical and lay literature about hyperactive children, but my wife, who had always been a good student, thought it was silly to even consider it. I hoped she was correct that Joshua would fit in a school the way she did instead of the way I didn't. But one thing was clear: The word *hyperactive* went very well with Joshua Roseman.

Soon Aaron was born, and Joshua and I were thrilled to have a new toy to play with. Joshua was great with Aaron and anticipated his every need. Joshua knew if Aaron wanted a certain toy or his bottle and always had the energy to go and fetch it for him. Ellen and I were relieved and gratified that Joshua was happy to pitch in and help care for little Aaron. We remembered how difficult it was to watch Joshua and actually have time for anything else. One thing was becoming clear however: There was a stark contrast between Joshua and Aaron.

Unlike Joshua, Aaron rarely moved in utero. Because Ellen had suffered a miscarriage between Aaron and Joshua we were always nervous about this lack of movement. Soon we found out that Ellen had diabetes, and we assumed that was the reason for the difference. But even when her blood sugars were controlled Aaron hardly moved. When he was born we were relieved that he was fine. Like Joshua, he never cried. Unlike Joshua, we could put him down on the floor in a certain spot and come back an hour later and he would still be there. He also slept later than Joshua, and he loved his crib. He did not want his own bed, and when we finally got him one because he was growing out of the crib, he fell out of it every single night. We simply put another mattress on the floor next to him in anticipation of his nightly roll out.

When it came time to send Joshua to school we considered my own past and Joshua's present. We knew we would have to look carefully for a school where he could prosper in a kind and nurturing environment, and one that could deal with his level of energy. We felt that a private school would be best because the teacher to pupil ratio would allow for more people to occupy and watch him. I did not want to take any chances.

We decided to apply for nursery school because my problems had started in kindergarten and I wanted to make the transition from nursery school to kindergarten and first grade easy for him. A clear choice emerged. There were certain buzzwords associated with every school and for this one the word was *Pluralism*. That meant that they encouraged diversity of thought and expression. It sounded great. It had a strong academic program and seemed to be a kind and nurturing place. An added bonus was that it provided religious training from an intellectual point of view without being overbearing. We liked everything we heard, and we heard a lot. We asked around and were told it was almost impossible to get accepted because there were just a few vacancies for hundreds of applicants.

We called the school to get an application and were informed that we could not have an application unless we first toured the school, so we scheduled a tour. On the appointed morning we dressed in our Sunday finest. This was difficult for me because I had to wear a suit. I was not comfortable in a suit.

Joshua, too, was bothered by clothing. He could not tolerate tags in his shirts; they drove him to distraction. We had to remove the tags or he would not wear them. I was the same way. They made me itchy and fidgety. But I could dress up when I had to.

Ellen dressed beautifully and was not fidgety. She was never fidgety. I knew that was a good thing. Although I felt bad about being fidgety, I couldn't help it. But I had learned to deal with it over the years.

We had not seen the school prior to the tour, and as we drove up we were impressed. As we stepped inside we were overwhelmed by the architectural detail. We were directed into a wood-paneled anteroom with a large and impressive fireplace.

We were immediately drawn to the children's work, which was displayed on the walls. The level of accomplishment of the students stunned us. This was a special place.

The children here were special and they were smart—very smart. We could see that from the compositions and the math projects. And the art was so beautiful it was almost too much to behold.

The parent volunteer who was responsible for our group approached us. She led us into an ornate wood-paneled room that was crowded with parents. Ellen did a quick mental calculation and whispered in my ear that there must have been at least five hundred applicants.

The tour was fascinating. We met the School Director and Department Heads and were exposed to our first discussion on "pluralism." This discussion meant that everybody's opinion would be heard and evaluated in the view that no single explanatory system or view of reality can account for all the phenomena of life.

Pluralism sounded good. Everybody was important. Everybody would have a voice. Everyone would be listened to with respect. I liked that. I had never had a voice in school; I was just a kid with a problem. No one listened to kids like us, and our parents just sort of hung their heads in shame.

During the tour, as we moved through the classrooms and the gym and the art room, and so on, we asked questions . . . and answered some. Each time someone said something the parent volunteer would write a note on a small index card. I could not believe they were evaluating us, but I reasoned that it was good. They wanted to know if the parents were people of substance, and as we looked around the room and conversed with the other parents we had a sudden realization. Everyone appeared to be very high functioning and driven. There were doctors, lawyers, investment bankers, and so on—and they appeared to be successful. Everybody was dressed very well. Everyone looked like they were going to work even though it was 6:00 P.M. Everyone carried a cell phone and a pager, and many had portable computers. I figured for sure that these people had sat in the front row when they were in school. I knew that Ellen had been a front rower. It made me nervous, like the enemy was surrounding me. But that was nothing new.

We knew it would be tough for Joshua to gain admittance and we realized that if he did not get in it would be not be a source of shame. There was simply too much competition.

After the tour we were given a mind-boggling form to fill out, which reminded me of a college application. There was no rush because it stated on the application: "Mail or bring to the interview." Nevertheless, I went to work on it as soon as we arrived home. "What important thing has your child learned, how did you teach it to him, and give examples?" This was intense for nursery school. I was up to it, though. I would do anything to make sure that Joshua did not have to live his own version of my school nightmare.

A few weeks later, I again had to dress up in uncomfortable clothes when we went for our parents' interview with the School Director. Again, we felt a rush as we entered the building, soaking up the wall displays the way you inhale in a terrific bakery.

As we entered the Director's Office and sat down I noticed index cards on her desk. I realized that those were the very same index cards our tour volunteer had been writing on.

In a stern but comforting voice she said, "You never sent in your application." I felt a sudden familiar pang of terror. Although I had done a great job on the application, I now realized that I had never mailed it in. I had goofed. I was sure all the other parents had mailed theirs. I was struck by a familiar feeling of being in the principal's office for doing something wrong because I did not understand the teacher. I was ready for the old lecture. As I considered how bad I was, I thought that Ellen would be furious with me. I was always forgetting to bring things with me, which was why I usually wore a pouch. Today, because I was wearing a suit I had left my pouch at home. I was sweating profusely and struggling to conceal my increasing panic.

"We have it right here," sang my wife in her lilting voice. "It said on the application we could bring it with us to the interview." Good move, I thought. Ellen was prepared. I knew from previous discussions that Ellen had always been the teacher's pet and a front row student precisely because she could always anticipate the teacher's needs. She was unlike me; I had rarely known what the teacher was talking about or wanted. It was clear that Ellen had anticipated the question, and as she handed the application over to the school's director I saw their eyes meet. I could tell that they understood and liked each other. I breathed a sigh of relief. I was glad Ellen was on my team.

Ellen was pleasant, as usual, and I let her answer most of the principal's questions, which she did with aplomb. It was clear that she, unlike me, felt comfortable in a school setting.

I was happy to see the School Director scrutinizing my responses. I had thought carefully about the questions, had spent a lot of time composing my answers, and I wanted to be appreciated. It was not lost on me, however, that while I had composed great answers, I would have flunked the interview because I would have forgotten to bring the application with me.

The interview was genial. She wanted information about us and Joshua and our commitment to this type of school and to our child. She was clear, however, in stating that there were very few available spaces and encouraged us to apply the next year. She explained that if our son was not accepted we should not take it personally. I told her I would not, but that we liked everything about the school and especially the pluralistic philosophy. I could not help but mention that Joshua would be an asset to any school. As we left the office we realized there was no way Joshua would be accepted to this school. The director had pretty much told us so, though not in so many words, but we really liked the place and we thought it would be interesting to see how things turned out.

Now that we had toured the school and filled out an application worthy of Harvard, it was time for Joshua to be evaluated. He had to go the school on a Sunday afternoon for his interview. We were somewhat concerned about the timing. After all, considering the competition, we wanted Joshua to be at his best, but the appointment was scheduled for the time he was usually napping or having his energetic spurt. We ultimately decided that I should not go to the interview because I am a nervous sort and because my experiences with the educational system had been less than stellar. Ellen, the school pro, was therefore designated to take Joshua. After all, she had a track record of being liked by teachers; I didn't.

Ellen arrived at the interview and found that Joshua was one of six or seven children to be evaluated at the same time. There were a number of teachers present. It was essentially playtime under a microscope. Ellen sat down and stayed out of the action. Joshua moved easily among the crowd of kids. He engaged the teachers and, as was his way, had a good time. He painted at the easel and made some clay snakes and a few other things. Some of the kids had problems with this test. Some children did not want to leave their mothers, some of the mothers forgot who the interview was for, and some kids were shy or just unable to connect. In other words, they were just a bunch of kids.

Ellen returned and recounted the interview in detail. Joshua had been himself—open, curious, friendly, and bright. We knew he was like this but it was nice to have some validation. Joshua was a star. We knew it. Now the school knew it. We still had no illusions about Joshua being accepted but we were proud of our boy, and I was encouraged by the way that Ellen and I complemented each other during the application process.

When Joshua was accepted we were shocked and honored. We had no idea that he was *such* a star. I felt great about the way my son was starting out in school. I figured for sure that he was taking after Ellen, and I heaved a big sigh of relief.

Ellen had a friend of fifteen years, with whom she was very close. We knew her child. He was nice and smart. When she called Ellen to discuss the acceptances she was upset. Her son was not accepted. Ellen did not know what to say. Her friend did.

"I can't believe it, my son is a lot smarter than Jos . . ." She caught herself, but the damage was done. Ellen was shocked. They stopped being friends after that. The insensitivity of the remark was what struck Ellen. I felt differently. I knew that her friend was a special education teacher, so her sense of entitlement to judge Joshua coupled with her lack of sensitivity unnerved me. It evoked memories of my own difficulties with teachers. She reminded me of my teachers. She always had. I again felt like that little boy who always seemed to be judged harshly by teachers. But this was different. This time it was about Joshua, and I did not like it. Ellen and I spoke about the comment and I related to her my feelings about a teacher making a comment like that about our son. Ellen felt that it was just a highly insensitive comment. She did not like the comment either, but she thought I was getting a bit carried away. I agreed. But perhaps that teacher saw something in Joshua, and perhaps I saw something in her. Regardless, it was clear that the school saw something in Joshua—they wanted him.

chapter two

Nursery School

Joshua loved nursery school and it loved him. He quickly made good friends, effortlessly striking up relationships with his classmates and their parents. Each morning, as he entered the classroom, he would greet his friends—parents and children—just like on the playground. None of the other kids connected with the parents in this way and we were proud of how mature and gregarious he was.

Believing that children should experience their first school separation from their parents in a relaxed and positive fashion, the school insisted that parents remain with their children in the classroom each day until their children were comfortable staying alone. The school determined "comfortable" by having parents ask their child if it was okay to leave and having the child say yes. For the first few days the shy or anxious children wanted their parents to stay until the end of class, but by the end of the first week almost the entire class was comfortable letting their parents leave. Joshua, despite being gregarious and self-assured, steadfastly refused to say yes. Initially he gave all sorts of reasons, like he was afraid, but usually he just shrugged his shoulders, and the teachers looked on to make sure we weren't pressuring him. This went on for three months. He gave no reasons—just shrugs.

We could have and would have left him. We were not pleased about allowing a three-year-old to manipulate us in this way. But we were so happy that the school was taking an interest in our son that we uncharacteristically abandoned our own good sense and judgment and acquiesced. Ellen and I, both strong personalities in our own lives, suddenly felt diffident and intimidated when it came to our son in school. Something about Joshua's behavior was out of kilter but we overlooked it because Joshua was bright, personable, and well behaved, and we were still thrilled to be the parents of a star.

Occasionally I would slowly edge toward the back of the room, and when I noticed that ten or fifteen minutes had elapsed without Joshua even glancing back at me, I would sneak out of the class without asking his permission. When I came to pick Joshua up after class he hadn't noticed I'd left and didn't mention it. He hadn't cried or looked for Ellen or me. But the teachers' upset that I was harming Joshua in some way scolded me. I pointed out that Joshua really did not mind if I left, that he only minded if I *asked* if I could leave. This sparked a meeting with the ECD (Early Childhood Director). The ECD agreed with the teachers, summarily dismissing my explanations.

As a physician, I was not used to having my opinions summarily dismissed. People sought my advice, hung on my every word, and considered my opinions carefully. But here my opinions were met with faint smiles and sympathetic looks, followed by "We are the professionals here, we know best." Or, "As a doctor, you do not let patients tell you what to do." I found this statement especially offensive. I always listened to my patients precisely because I had seen other doctors miss a diagnosis for disregarding patient's insights. Patients would sometimes disagree with me, and I would sometimes say, "Okay, let's try it your way for a brief period and see, and then if it doesn't work let's try it my way." But I was finding out that teachers always thought they were right.

The Early Childhood Director (ECD) spoke to us about this problem. We were surprised to hear it referred to as a problem. Ellen and I were convinced that the school was allowing our child to manipulate us, but the ECD reassured us that she had dealt with separation issues like this before and that this approach would help him begin his school life on the right foot. Given my problems at school I was struck with pangs of guilt every time she said something like that.

I did not want Joshua to start out the way that I had. Many patients had sought my guidance on such issues, and I had told them that as parents they should insist that their opinions be taken into account. I had marveled at how helpless people had usually felt when I said this. Suddenly I felt helpless and I wasn't quite sure why.

I spoke to Ellen and some other parents about what I considered a lack of intellectual curiosity and accountability on the part of the teachers and the ECD. I quickly realized that people assumed that there was something wrong with Joshua and me for considering that the teachers were not perfect. I was becoming known as a malcontent and people assumed that was why Joshua had this separation issue.

I had heard people rant about how the schools smugly ignored them and had assumed that these parents were simply unreasonable. Now I took the time to reconsider those previous conversations, and began asking more pointed questions of the dissatisfied parents. It was becoming clear to me that this was a pervasive problem. I concluded that the educators were generally rigid, and even where individual teachers were willing to adapt they were prevented from doing so by the system. I had eerily reminiscent feelings from my childhood, like a "bad boy" being scolded by teachers, yet I repressed my natural inclination to fight because I didn't want to ruin anything for Joshua. Ellen and I became fixtures in the class. The teachers loved having us; we befriended the other kids and did what we could to help the teachers. I enjoyed interacting with the children, and I found the teacher-student interaction fascinating and instructive. One of the mothers mentioned to Ellen that she felt sorry for me, assuming that I was unemployed. But I was simply determined to do whatever it took to spare Joshua from a dysfunctional school experience like my own.

Finally, around Thanksgiving, Joshua allowed us to leave. The teachers and the Early Childhood Director were thrilled and assured us that we had done the right thing. When I considered how happy they were and how they dealt with the problem, I should have been forewarned. I felt they were making a mountain out of a molehill and it made me nervous to think what they would do with a mountain. I would soon find out.

As the year progressed, aside from the separation issue Joshua seemed like a bright and personable child. He loved school, and never missed a day. His speech development was a bit slow, and the teachers spoke to us about that. We explained that this didn't concern us because Ellen and my brother Jeffrey had not spoken until they were four years of age. In Ellen's case, she just started speaking in complete sentences. My final comment on the matter, stolen from my grandmother, was, "He will know how to talk before he walks down the aisle."

Sure enough, as the school year drew to a close, the teachers informed us that there had been a dramatic improvement in Joshua's speech during the last few months and they were no longer concerned about his speech development. We were glad to hear that they were no longer concerned about something we were never concerned about to begin with. We were content, and so was Joshua.

chapter three

Problems Arise

In Pre-K Joshua loved going to school. We saw him learning all kinds of things and were impressed by his expanding and interesting vocabulary. But he was becoming increasingly difficult for everyone but me to understand. He confused genders. He often called me Mommy and Ellen Daddy—though there was no particular pattern. Up and down were confused, and right and left made no sense to him at all. He talked about things in a way that was fascinating but odd. He could describe an airplane in a way that was almost poetic, but he was unable to actually say the word *airplane*. There were many other words that he had trouble recalling. As he searched for a word he began to stammer. Soon he was stammering all the time. Many people found this annoying; I looked at it differently, perhaps because I possessed this same peculiarity.

Context and body language had always been more important to me than specific words. While I appreciated the specificity of words, I was forced to develop the ability to describe things in a multitude of ways. Sometimes there was a word on the tip of my tongue and I simply could not remember it. It was as if the word was locked in an impenetrable safe in my head. Crucial to my overcoming this condition was accepting my inability to retrieve a word, and quickly moving on by substituting another word. I had become so good at it that hardly anyone noticed. Watching Joshua I realized that it had helped my speaking skills by forcing me to enlarge my vocabulary. I now saw this happening in Joshua with his ever-increasing and interesting vocabulary. I explained to him that I found it fascinating watching his speech develop. I also reinforced that even though he stammered now, one day he would be a great speaker just like his daddy because of the skills he was acquiring. So every time Joshua could not find a word, I encouraged him to move on quickly to a new word and not feel bad about his stammering. I explained that while it might not be normal for most people, it was normal for him and me, and he shouldn't worry about it. I showed him how word retrieval problems still happen to me under many circumstances by playing a videotape for him. Joan Lunden was interviewing me in front of a live studio audience. I explained to him that because I had been on TV many times

I was not nervous, so that could not explain my trouble finding words. We watched together as I explained.

The show opened and as I sat down across from Miss Lunden, her astonishing beauty suddenly overwhelmed me. While not struck dumb, I was suddenly having a difficult time finding my words. My experience with retrieving words had given me a vast vocabulary base and the ability to interchange words quickly and without detection, however, so Joshua did not see me stammer. I explained to him that one day he would be just like me, and he would not stammer either. Joshua understood that.

Aside from the stammering, Joshua's speech was becoming more difficult to understand because of what his teacher referred to as sequencing. He gave out lots of information but he would say things out of order or at inappropriate times. However, he had an extraordinary ability to see connections that others did not. His manner of explaining them was cryptic, to be sure, but because of our similarity I had no trouble following him. It was clear to me that he was just having a number of running conversations in his brain at the same time and sometimes confused them.

It was old news that Joshua understood me when others did not and vice versa. The most important reason for this was that we were perpetually engaged in nonverbal communication. A quick glance to the right might mean I was looking for something; stopping for a moment to listen to a sound would often tip Joshua off that someone was expected; or a body lean might mean I was going to raid the refrigerator. We spent lots of time studying each other and anticipating each other's movements in our own personal secret game. Some people were amazed at our apparent clairvoyance. My personal opinion was that the two of us were always restless and we amused ourselves by studying each other and carrying on numerous verbal and nonverbal conversations. Our minds were often wandering so we would just pick up or drop off where we could. Attention did not matter in our secret game. In fact, it made it even more fun. "That boy is just like his daddy, and he just likes his daddy," someone said. It never occurred to me that this was anything to be worried about.

At the first parent-teacher conference, Joshua's teacher mentioned that she thought he had several speech issues such as stammering and sequencing. I was not surprised. I explained that Ellen and I had noticed, as had everyone else, but we were not overly concerned. It was slightly annoying, but just one of those things. I pointed out that I had had a succession of bad habits as a kid and they had passed. I also mentioned that as a physician I had said, to the relief of countless new mothers, "Boys stammer, girls don't. It usually goes away, and even when girls *do* stammer it usually goes away." I thought that covered the issue of stammering and I was satisfied. I dismissed the sequencing issue in the same way.

His teacher also expressed concern about Joshua's energy level, noting that he seemed to be in perpetual motion, unable to sit still for even a brief period. I explained my hypothesis on energy. People drink coffee to get it. TV tells kids to eat candy bars to get it. People take pills to get it. Joshua was lucky to have it. I had always firmly believed energy to be the secret of most success, and Joshua had it in abundance.

After the conference we were referred to the Early Childhood Director again. She remembered us from the previous year when she had pressured us into staying in the back of Joshua's class to deal with his "separation anxiety." She remembered and liked Joshua. Joshua, Ellen, and I liked her a lot. She was extremely nice, but as tensions escalated and Joshua's problems grew, I became more and more disenchanted with the school and its approach to teaching.

She suggested that holding Joshua back might help. In these situations, "it is always good for boys to be left back," she said. Because Joshua was one of the youngest kids in the class it made some sense, but Ellen and I were surprised. While we realized that Joshua had some speech peculiarities and an extra year might allow him to improve, we didn't think he would be left back. The stammering may have annoyed others, but even with his disordered sentences and word retrieval problems, he could make himself understood; it just took longer. Nevertheless, Ellen and I explained that we appreciated her candor and concern and told her that we would think about and discuss it.

Over the next few months Ellen and I were more critical of Joshua than we had ever been before. We were looking for clues that would indicate that there was some type of problem that would require him to be left back. We discussed it and agonized over it, and finally both of us came to the same conclusion. If Joshua's teacher felt it was appropriate to leave him back we would agree.

Joshua's teacher, Patty, was wonderful. She was caring, insightful, sweet, and experienced. We trusted her implicitly. She made it abundantly clear that she loved Joshua and thought he was a very special child despite his hyperactivity and speech problems. She pointed out that he had a kind and gentle nature, which made him a great asset to the class. She said that she would monitor the situation closely and discuss it with the Early Childhood Director.

We made another appointment with the ECD after her discussion with Patty. She explained that she thought we should have Joshua tested by a specialist. I was prepared for that, based on the large number kids in my practice who were referred for testing and therapies, when I did not see the need for it. I mentioned to Ellen that I had very serious reservations about testing, but it was more than that. In discussing a specialist, no mention was ever made of a physician, such as a developmental pediatrician or psychiatrist. I realize that I have a certain prejudice, but when I think of the word *specialist* I usually think of the word *doctor* connected to it. I realized that there were reading specialists, and language specialists, and lots of other specialists, but I was still surprised that when they said specialist, they never meant a physician.

An interesting situation was emerging. Ellen felt that we

should follow the suggestions of the school personnel, including consulting their specialists. As far as she could see, there was nothing seriously wrong with Joshua, and her experience in school had led her to believe that things always worked out fine. I disagreed. My experience in school led me to expect the worst. I considered her point of view, but the fact was, I did not trust school personnel to make decisions about my son. I reminded Ellen about the separation fiasco of the previous year. She reminded me that it had all worked out just fine. Touché.

I was beginning to feel isolated and alone. Ellen did not feel it. She had never had bad feelings about school, and therefore could not understand what I was so worried about. The situation was beginning to create sides—and Ellen was leaning toward theirs. I felt just like I did when I was kid: It was the teachers against me.

Ellen was convinced there was nothing terribly wrong with Joshua, but she was starting to think there was something wrong with me. After all, I was still carrying a grudge against my first grade teacher. Long suppressed but familiar feelings weighed me down. I began remembering events from my childhood I thought I had long since buried, among them flashbacks of the day I got the report card that showed I had been left back. I relived the shame and hurt of that painful experience.

It was the last day of school at PS 221 in 1954. The first grade class was giddy, anticipating summer vacation, and I was a little giddier than the rest of the kids. I felt like a rocket ship about to blast off, barely able to contain myself and unable to stay in my seat. My teacher had positioned me in the last row because of my inability to contain myself, but that just made me worse.

Suddenly the class froze in anxious anticipation as the teacher began handing out the report cards. Four report cards were handed to the first kid in every row. Each kid methodically received and passed the report cards in a mesmerizing staccato rhythm, back to the kid behind him. Breaking the trance-like rhythmic movements of my row mates, I lunged for my report card and quickly opened it and scanned my grades. I stood uncharacteristically still and felt a sinking feeling in the pit of my stomach. At the bottom of my report card it read PROMOTED TO *grade 1*. Stealing glances at the ocean of undulating report cards around me confirmed my worst fear: They all had *grade 2* in the space where I had *grade 1*.

Confused, upset, fighting back tears, and carefully concealing my report card, I made my way through the semihysterical mass of five year olds. As I approached my teacher, I blurted out, "I think there is a mistake on my report card. It says PROMOTED TO *grade 1* here and I should be going into *grade 2*."

Standing perfectly still and scrutinizing my teacher's face before me, I saw *it*. I wasn't quite sure what *it* was, but I understood enough to recognize that *it* was "The Look."

"The Look" wasn't dominated by any particular facial feature. It was the way everything in the face worked in concert:

the furrowed brow, the eyes—slightly narrowed but not quite squinting, blazing with intense dislike, almost a revulsion, the lips pursed and moist. "The Look" pierced my soul and I froze. I became increasingly uncomfortable as I struggled to understand what was happening. I wasn't sure if I wanted to scream or cry. I remember it to this day, more than forty years later, in vivid detail because I have seen "The Look" so many times since.

The teacher peered down at me for a long moment. Then, ever so slowly, she lowered her head until she was directly opposite me, only inches away, and said, "There is no mistake." I shuddered as I felt the impact of the horrible truth. Containing my feelings of shame and humiliation, I moved quickly toward the door and slipped out quietly onto the street.

I burst through the door of my apartment. My mother was waiting, as usual, and I immediately relieved myself of the horrible truth. I had been left back.

Suddenly my mother was sobbing uncontrollably. I felt horrible in a new way. Not only was I hurt but my mother appeared to be mortally wounded. This was going to be very, very bad, I thought. I realized for the first time what a tragedy this was. This was just like a funeral I had seen, where everybody was speaking in whispers and crying, and my *father* hadn't even gotten home yet. I told my mother that I had known I was not doing well, but I didn't think I would be *left back*. Suddenly my hysterical mother blurted, "You are not *really* being left back. Your teacher just did that because you don't listen to her in class. You don't pay attention. You're always daydreaming and forgetting things and you don't sit still. She thought this would teach you a lesson." I stared at my mother in stunned silence, not knowing what to say. It was a lesson all right. I learned very clearly that day who the enemy was. The lines were drawn: teachers on one side and me on the other.

Even at that tender age I understood the unbelievable cruelty of what that teacher had done. She wanted to hurt me and she wanted me to know it. I was being punished for *what* I was. I could never sit still, yet that day I had been stilled. I rarely paid attention, yet that day she had my undivided and absolute attention. I had stood paralyzed and riveted.

In Joshua's case, the Early Childhood Director continued to recite the educators' mantra: "It is good to leave a boy back, and they never even notice after the first week." We knew, however, that Joshua *would* notice and in fact would be mortified. I remembered the threat of being left back in first grade. The very thought of it was almost too painful to think about, even now. I wondered how they could be so insensitive to a child's feelings.

We became hesitant to speak to other parents in Joshua's class, not wanting to get too close in case Joshua was left back. We wanted Joshua to develop some new friends, just in case. But Joshua loved the friends he had.

Ultimately Ellen had faith in the school personnel. She

began reminding me that Joshua was not me. I, however, was thinking just the opposite.

We decided to do it the school's way, after all. How bad could it be? My wife was comfortable with it, and I did not want to appear unreasonable. They were experts. We decided to get a full evaluation. We were referred to an expert who seemed eminently qualified, from her business card. It read:

DR. E, PH.D.
LICENSED PSYCHOLOGIST.
LEARNING DISABILITIES SPECIALIST
LICENSED SPEECH LANGUAGE PATHOLOGIST.

She looked good on paper.

chapter four

Experts and Specialists

Dr. E wanted to interview Ellen and me prior to Joshua's evaluation. As is my custom, we arrived at her office early. She called us in ten minutes past the appointment time.

Her office was a spare but pleasant room. Off to the right was a wooden children's table with two matching chairs neatly placed underneath. Straight ahead was an immaculate, uncluttered wood desk backlit by sunlight streaming through a large picture window. To the left, just in front of the desk, were a small, well-worn dark sofa and a large leather easy chair arranged around a coffee table smeared with many fingerprints. Dr. E directed us toward the sofa. As we sat down, the sofa burped and we sank into it quickly and uncomfortably. Dr. E then collapsed with a gigantic thud into the big easy chair, facing us.

In stark contrast to her office, she looked anything but neat. She wore slightly ill-fitting but fashionable black clothing that looked as though it had been slept in. Her round face, with little makeup, appeared to have just awakened from the same nap as her clothing. Her hair was clean but in disarray. She clutched a large, yellow-lined pad, and then ceremoniously placed it on her lap, causing a loud thud. She began to tap her ornate black and gold pen, her body gyrating in perfect concert to its rhythm, and she nodded repeatedly, as if agreeing with herself as she spoke. I found her constant shifting positions in her chair and her way of rapidly moving her hands very distracting.

Suddenly Dr. E stopped tapping and began asking direct questions in a staccato rhythm. First she fired off some general questions about Joshua, which Ellen answered with her usual aplomb, and then she moved on to questions about Joshua's problems. Ellen hesitated momentarily as I explained that while we had noticed Joshua's stammering, speech eccentricities, and slow but steadily developing speech, we did not consider it a problem until school officials pointed it out. Dr. E gripped her pen tightly and furiously scribbled every word we said on her pad. Like an abstract artist painting a canvas, she wrote in one spot, then another, moving back and forth with a stroke here, one there, and back again.

Next she asked whether we had speech problems. Ellen explained that she did not speak until the age of four, at which time she started speaking in complete sentences. I explained that my brother also did not speak until age four, and that I, too, mixed genders, confused words, and suffered through periods of stammering in my life. I added that I considered myself to have ADD and some learning problems, though they were untreated and I had overcome them.

Dr. E was fascinated by my story and how I overcame my problems. She also discussed her own learning and attention problems, which, she pointed out, she had not yet fully overcome. I was uncomfortable with her confession. My understanding was that psychologists should keep their personal lives private. I did not want to know about her disabilities. I also felt that she should make a totally objective assessment of Joshua and did not want my background to prejudice her conclusions in any way. Nevertheless, I reluctantly conceded the logic of these questions because, as a doctor, I believed strongly in taking a careful family history, and could understand how grasping the scope of my problems might give her insight into Joshua and his problems. It also made sense that her own personal experience would aid her in diagnosing and treating people who were somewhat different, and that she wanted to share that knowledge with us.

As the interview drew to a close, we had clarified two things: I had learning disabilities, and Dr. E had learning disabilities. She was assuming that Joshua had the same thing that we had. She explained that she would perform an "exhaustive battery of tests," compile and analyze the data, and then have us back to discuss the results. So far, so good.

A few days later Ellen and I accompanied Joshua to his first appointment. After racing up two flights of steps, we were glad to enter the office and sit down. Joshua, as usual, did not feel any need to rest. As he jumped around, looking at and touching everything, I realized that we had hardly noticed the waiting area before. It was small, but more importantly, there was nothing for him to do in that space. We thought it was odd that a waiting room for children did not have any games, books, or toys to occupy waiting time.

Dr. E emerged from her room ten minutes late and motioned for Joshua to enter. I asked if I could observe and she nodded yes. Joshua and I crossed the threshold, leaving Ellen behind. I knew that Ellen always wanted to be included in everything, and respected her insight and would have welcomed her involvement. However, everything happened so quickly, and Dr. E did not say anything, so I decided I would explain everything to Ellen later in great detail.

I was directed to the burping sofa and Joshua to the small wooden children's table, where he and Dr. E sat down facing each other. Dr. E noticed Joshua was uncomfortable so she gave him a toy, let him play with it for a few moments, smiled, and began the testing. I sat down on the small sofa, heard the burp, and sank physically and emotionally.

I moved over to Joshua to rub his back in the hope that it would help him focus on the test. Dr. E caught my eye and nodded, letting me know that she thought it was a good idea. Joshua noticed her nod and then looked up at me, trying to figure out what was going on. I could see that he was struggling with the questions because he was getting increasingly fidgety.

Her manner of asking questions, staring at Joshua waiting for a response, and then looking disappointed with the response appeared to be influencing Joshua. I could see his body tense and his head dart around, looking for an escape, after each incorrect answer. The questions were of the kind that I remembered from my childhood testing. They were about putting things in order by height or size and identifying patterns from groups of circles or squares or triangles.

I could understand Joshua's negative reponse to nonverbal pressure to perform. Anyone would feel that way with someone hovering judgmentally over him or her. As I sat rubbing Joshua's back, I peeked over his shoulder, mentally taking the test myself. I had trouble understanding most of the questions, much less knowing the correct answers. I was relieved when Dr. E suddenly said, "Let's end early today and start fresh next time." Aha! I thought to myself, she possessed insight. Perhaps I had judged her too hastily. Perhaps she was just having a bad day, or Joshua was, or I was. (Of course Joshua and I were fine until we got in there, and the testing itself only lasted about ten minutes.)

The next meeting, a few days later, started the same way except that Dr. E was later than usual and by the time we entered the room, both Joshua and I were in "Attentional Hyperspace," a dreamy state in people with ADD where all attention is lost. Dr. E started the testing, and once again I rubbed Joshua's back and glanced over his shoulder, mentally taking the test along with him. It was clear that neither of us could figure out which way the triangles went or how to separate the squares or order sequences of weird pictures. Also Dr. E was sitting opposite us and working backward which was confusing to me and, I assumed, to Joshua also. Once again her movements were distracting.

I considered the possibility that both Joshua and I had the same problem and that was the reason we were both having such a hard time with the test. However, I also reasoned that a forty-five-year-old physician should be capable of taking a test aimed at a child in nursery school.

At the next meeting Dr. E. showed up without her keys, which caused us to start late. She never showed up for the meeting after that.

The entire process was an eye-opening experience for me as a doctor, and a heart-wrenching experience as a parent. The professional demeanor of Dr. E shocked me. But even more disturbing was the manner in which the test was administered, and its content. As a doctor I questioned the test's reliability and validity. Reliability is the degree of dependability of a measuring instrument. Ideally results of a particular test should be reproducible. The test may be given under a variety of circumstances, but the results should always be the same—with different testers, in different rooms, and in different parts of the country. It should not matter whether the test is given by Dr. E or by a practitioner in Duluth. In Joshua's case, the fact that, he was uncomfortable with the tester meant that he would probably perform differently with a different tester. What did this mean for the reliablity of the test?

Asking Joshua questions about triangles and squares and sequencing in a pressurized environment did not, in my mind, accurately assess Joshua's intellectual ability. It might be useful with certain kinds of children, but not with slightly unusual children like Joshua.

Prior to the last session, I sought to find out how much was known about Learning Disabilities and Attention Deficit Disorder (ADD). As I read, talked to colleagues and spoke to some other specialists, I found that my initial belief—that effective diagnostic and treatment procedures were firmly in place—was more wishful than accurate. I came upon a recent report by the National Institutes of Health (NIH), which called Attention Deficit Disorder a "profound problem," noting that over a million children take powerful drugs to control it. The report stated that reliable methods of diagnosing and treating the disorder remain "elusive." Said the panel chairman: "There is no current, validated diagnostic test" for Attention Deficit Disorder. Another panelist spoke more bluntly: "Diagnosis is a mess."

This raised a second issue. Was the test valid? Did the test really test what it was supposed to? I thought not. So I had come to the conclusion from a scientific perspective that the test lacked reliability and validity.

As a family practitioner, I often take a critical view of specialist-oriented medicine. I do not like it when my patients are sent for unnecessary tests, put to extra expense in time or money, or treated insensitively. I accept that good bedside manner is becoming a lost art, but what I saw here and what I would continue to see as the process evolved was far beyond what I had ever imagined possible.

Ellen, somewhat incredulous of my findings and opinions, understood my reluctance to attend the last session or the final meeting with Dr. E. She took Joshua to the last session alone, and promised to stop by my office later to tell me the results. Less than two hours later Ellen burst into my office, distraught and hysterical. Tears streaming down her face, she sank into a chair, held her head in her hands, and sobbed. I stood frozen with fear, expecting to hear catastrophic news. Barely audible through her sobs I heard her say, "I just came from Dr. E's office and she told me the results of her evaluation. It was horrible; I felt as if she was telling me my baby had cancer, I know I shouldn't feel that way because he is healthy and he's a nice boy but I just can't help it."

As Ellen sat there holding her head in her hands and sobbing, I considered her comment about our son: healthy and nice. I had heard patients speak that way about a family member with significant mental or emotional disabilities. It was a step along the path of coming to terms with diminished expectations and guilt. Nothing we had seen in Joshua suggested anything of such magnitude.

I knew Ellen wanted me to sit down next to her, put my arms around her, and tell her that we could handle it together, reassure her that everything would be all right. Although I would have liked to have done that I could not because of my personal history. Instead I launched into an angry diatribe about Dr. E, the school administrators who had referred us to her, and my own childhood. I accused Ellen of previously consorting with the enemy, and now joining them. As proof, I pointed to the fact that she had accepted that something was wrong with Joshua. My parents felt there was something wrong with me, and felt a sense of disappointment and guilt. I did not and would not ever feel that way about Joshua. He was fine, I knew it, and I was disappointed in her being swayed by others.

I felt almost immediate remorse for my uncharacteristic outburst. My wife had never been my enemy. We had disagreements, but she was always on my side. She was also on Joshua's side. I knew that she loved him deeply, no matter how exasperating he was or what anybody said about him. Yet she was looking at this from a very different perspective from mine.

Ellen had grown up trusting the educational establishment and, as a result, trusted these experts and school personnel. She had no reason to disbelieve them or their

methods. At every level of her educational process, including college and work, she had mentors urging her on to bigger and better things and taking pride in her considerable
achievements. Ellen simply could not fathom that the system
that had cherished her and served her so well could be so
wrong when it came to Joshua. She trusted them because
they had always been kind to her. But I had never known
that kindness.

I had always seen teachers and the rest of the educational
establishment as the enemy. I did not know the answers to
the teachers' questions, and was often humiliated for not
even knowing the question. So it was quite natural for me
to jump to the conclusion that teachers could be horrible
monsters who were torturing my son. They had done it to
me, and I had seen them do it to others.

I was astounded at the reaction of my heretofore confident, successful, independent-minded wife, and I was dumbfounded that she could be so terribly upset. I had seen her
handle much worse than this without being rattled. I had
often joked that I was married to "Prozac" because of Ellen's
unflappable demeanor. I had never seen her get truly upset
about anything. In fact, at the end of her pregnancy with
Joshua, while I was a nervous wreck worrying about every
conceivable complication, Ellen summed up her attitude by
saying "I am prepared for and expect the best, but can handle the worst." I found great comfort in those words, and
had quoted them often to appreciative patients. It was a cap-

sule summary of Ellen's attitude about life. Where, I wondered, was that attitude now?

I rested my case with the query, "Do you think that Joshua could have a horrible developmental abnormality and I, a physician, never noticed?"

When I saw Ellen glaring up at me from the office chair, I knew I was in trouble. My wife had always had the greatest respect for me as a physician. Now I saw doubt in her eyes; I had never seen that before. She knew how felt I about this. She knew that if I had spent twenty minutes with a patient and missed a diagnosis of this magnitude, I would consider myself guilty of malpractice.

I asked her again, "Do you believe that it's even remotely possible I overlooked a pervasive developmental disorder in Joshua?" Again she stared back at me. That stare pierced my soul. I considered my devotion to my family one of the unassailable truths in my life, and was absolutely confident that I would have noticed a problem. I was shocked that Ellen could even consider the possibility that I might not.

As I looked at Ellen, her eyes swollen and red from crying, looking defeated, I had an eerie feeling of déjà vu. This was exactly what I had promised myself I would never allow: for my family and my son, disabled or not, to suffer the way my family and I had when I was a young boy.

I decided to speak to Dr. E personally, and Ellen and I went over together. I was totally unprepared for what she was about to tell me. Looking straight into my eyes, Dr. E spoke very slowly. "It's bad. Very bad. Worse than I ever thought."

I felt as if I had been shot, and while I was still recoiling from the first impact, she fired again.

"He has a pan-developmental disorder. It will be very difficult for him to read, ever. As for next year, when they say 'p' is 'puh,' he won't even know what they are talking about."

I could hardly believe what I was hearing. That dismal diagnosis, reserved for only the most severely affected children, meant Joshua was lagging behind in every single mental category. Then she followed that up by saying, "His IQ is so low it is unmeasurable."

I was stunned. We accepted that perhaps Joshua had some speech problems. His speech, while slow to develop, was improving, and he was capable of carrying on a conversation with his classmates, his teachers, and us. He confused genders, up and down, left and right, in and out, and, stammered. Speaking was a struggle for him, but he still did it unselfconsciously. His level of energy might be considered hyperactive, but he got along well with people, and was always pleasant at home and with his friends.

Dr. E recommended a speech therapist. We made no attempt to contact her because we were still traumatized by the testing. Days later, a woman called from a distant city and spoke with a thick foreign accent. She explained that she was a speech therapist, and had been asked by Dr. E. to call.

"How can you teach speech therapy in our city when you live three hours away?" I asked.

"I come down a couple of days a week," she answered.

I had serious reservations about whether speech therapy could be taught by a person with a thick foreign accent. Remembering how confusing the battery of tests had been, I decided that I did not want to expose Joshua to another bewildering situation. I felt this would be one more thing to fluster him. I was already critical of the reliability and validity of the test. I was struck by how everything seemed to center on the needs of the teachers, experts, and specialists, and how little attention was paid to the needs of the child. I was diplomatic, but clear that we were not interested.

The school still felt very strongly that Joshua needed speech therapy for his stammering, which we realized was increasing. We searched for a speech therapist with the school's help and by canvassing other parents. We called ten therapists, and every single one told us that they were simply too busy to take any more patients. Ellen and I wondered, could there be an epidemic of speech disorders that we had missed? I kept up with the medical journals, and would not have missed such an pervasive problem. I even went so far as to check MEDLINE, the comprehensive database of medical journals. Nothing there, either. This epidemic of speech disorders, it seemed, had been totally overlooked by the medical establishment.

We finally found a speech therapist through a friend of

Ellen's. I was surprised by the strong visceral response she elicited in me. She reminded me of everything I had always resented about teachers. She seemed rigid, judgmental, and supercilious. Nevertheless, I stayed out of her way and allowed her to work with Joshua—but things were not going well. Joshua absolutely refused to work with her. I was aghast. Ellen and I were strict parents and insisted on a certain code of conduct. We had never seen anything like that with Joshua.

The speech therapist approached me and said she wanted to discuss Joshua's stuttering. "No," I said, "he stammers. Boys often stammer, girls usually do not. It usually goes away." As a family doctor, I had said these exact words so many times to parents, it was an automatic response. I had seen stammering and I had seen stuttering, and I knew that Joshua was stammering. I could see him start to say something and forget what he was talking about, or see his mind wander. I knew that this was stammering. Stutterers do not stutter because they forget what they are talking about, and they do not stutter because their mind wanders. She looked at me sadly and said, "No, I'm afraid this is stuttering, and you need to accept that. But I think that he can be helped." As a parent, hearing something like that is a scary thing. Although the distinctions between stammering and stuttering are still controversial in the literature, it felt to me that she was telling me that Joshua had a much worse problem than I thought, and she was implying that I was in denial, which could possibly hurt my son. I wondered, Whatever happened to listening to the parents?

Over the years I had learned to respect parental intuition. I listened respectfully and carefully when parents, usually mothers, told me about their worries. I considered what they said carefully and always left some ray of hope. As a physician I was appalled at the way I was treated by the speech therapist, but as a parent I panicked. I was suddenly struck with a familiar sick feeling in the pit of my stomach. It was exactly the way I had felt when, as a child, my teachers spoke to me in a foreboding tone. I considered the prospect that I might be damaging my son for life. My mind raced; I remembered that my cousin stuttered. He was an unhappy fellow, never married, never smiled. Could I be wrong about Joshua? Could I be in denial? I had seen the tendency to deny or discount bad news many times with patients. Denial is powerful and insidious. Denial can kill. I know that. I was now worried that I was in denial about Joshua's possible impairment. Could Ellen and all of the professionals be right? I was thrown into complete disarray. The intuition, judgment, and stubborn determination that had gotten me this far deserted me. I agreed to do whatever she asked. "Do not," she said, "be around when we are working."

I agreed. The next week when she arrived I sat in the kitchen, reading in silence. Joshua ran from the room saying he would not work with her. She came in to talk to me about it. To my shock and amazement, she said that the reason that Joshua was not responding to the speech therapy was me.

"How could that be? I was out of the room."

"Your very presence upsets him. But that is not really the big problem."

"What, pray tell, *is* the big problem?" I asked, getting just a bit sarcastic.

"You don't really believe this will work, do you?"

"No," I said.

"Well, if you do not really believe, then it won't work."

It seemed ridiculous to me, and I responded, "So not only do I have to sit in the kitchen in silence and pay the bill, but I have to believe. Is that it?"

"Yes."

When Ellen got home, she called the therapist and left a message on her machine, telling her not to return. I could not make that call. I was too upset.

Was my desire to raise the perfect child at war with my reason? Was I so strongly in denial that I could jeopardize Joshua's well-being? Was I hearing stammering when he was actually stuttering because I couldn't accept the latter? Finally, I thought, was my hatred of these experts based on my own childhood and clouding my judgment? Was this about Joshua or about me? I was so conflicted; I simply withdrew and asked Ellen to make the decisions. I knew she would do whatever she believed was in Joshua's best interest regardless of what it meant to her own self-esteem. As always, she had hoped for the best, but I knew she was prepared to deal with the worst.

Ellen insisted on one more try with another therapist. Joshua liked this one much better, and after five or six sessions the therapist thought everything was going well. Then Joshua refused to work with him. Finally I came to my senses. It was possible for me to separate the professional from the personal. I was not in denial. I realized that what I had suspected was true. Forty years hadn't made a bit of difference; I was not going to accept any blame here and would not allow them to foist the blame on Joshua, either.

As the school year drew to a close, we had one last meeting with Joshua's teacher, Patty. She said she thought that it was important for the class and for Joshua that he not be left back, that he had become an integral part of the class, and that he would be very upset at being held back. She felt that he was a bright boy, and that it would all work out with the proper care. She also said that she was sorry that we had gotten a total evaluation instead just a speech evaluation and that things had gotten out of hand. We were relieved. She had truly been a beacon of light in the fog.

As we headed into the summer, Ellen and I were drained from the ordeal with the expert, speech therapists, and school. We avoided any conversations about Joshua's supposed problems. We needed time to look within ourselves for answers. One thing that we both agreed on, however, was that we were unhappy with the tumult created by the experts. We both felt that with all the attention and energy being concentrated on Joshua we were shortchanging Aaron; we were determined to throw ourselves into Joshua *and* Aaron that summer.

Aaron was now walking and starting to understand the world around him. He was much easier to care for than Joshua had been. He seemed to understand things quickly, and Ellen had more patience with him than she ever had with Joshua. Joshua went to camp and had a great summer; at camp there were no questions about him. He was a great athlete, a pleasant boy, and he talked a little funny. No one minded.

I, however, was upset that Ellen, being more relaxed with Aaron, seemed to be more patient with him. She accused me of favoring Joshua, which hurt me terribly, and I then accused her of favoring Aaron. Neither of us was correct. We loved both of our children, but we were a family in crisis. I remembered what that was like. I also knew that this scene was being played out in a multitude of homes across the country. There were many kids like Joshua and so many families frayed and battered because of it. It took a toll on us.

Ellen and I talked about the kids and spent lots of time with them, but we barely communicated with each other on a personal level. I spent more than a few nights sleeping on the sofa in the basement or on the boys' bunk beds. I knew that this upset Ellen. It seemed to me that she was leaning toward joining the enemy. To her I was exhibiting strange and unusual behavior. Although our personal relationship was falling apart, we had a great summer with the kids. We went places and spent lots of time playing with them. Whatever our problems, we were determined not to let the children suffer because of it.

Then came kindergarten.

chapter five

Kindergarten

Kindergarten started badly. Joshua loved it anyway. He was thrilled to be back at school, see his old friends, and meet his new teachers. During the first weeks, Joshua would arrive home and regale us with stories. He loved his new teachers and thought they were very smart. He also told us of all the new things he was learning, such as games, sports, and cooking. Suddenly we had a sparkling, if stammering, conversationalist on our hands, and Ellen and I enjoyed it immensely.

In sharp contrast to Joshua's cheerful descriptions of school, his teachers presented us with a different and darker view. All were concerned about him. Some children, they said, were making fun of Joshua's ever-present stammer, and in frustration Joshua had responded with his fists. We were shocked. Joshua, though energetic, had always had a gentle disposition.

Another problem was that he addressed his teachers as "teacher" rather than by their names. He often used descriptive terms when he was unable to think of a specific word. One of his teachers found this offensive and wondered about his attitude. The others spoke to us about his having a "word retrieval problem."

On the playground he referred to the other children as "boy" or "girl" rather than by their names. Other children didn't seem to mind. He played for hours with a multitude of children without ever uttering anyone's name. Joshua also could not recall the names of objects and would come up with descriptions or pantomime to convey his thoughts. Perhaps we had blinders on, but we saw his integration of descriptive terms and pantomime as indicative of emerging creativity. In class, however, when Joshua could not remember names of things it was perceived as a problem by his teachers. For instance, Joshua could not learn the days of the week. Each day was the same to him, so he referred to them as "day." He further described them as white or black, referring to days and nights. He understood yesterday, but the future was confusing, so he said "the other kind of yesterday." The beauty of his expression touched me. It was poetic and philosophical. Joshua's teachers had a different opinion.

The teachers felt that Joshua was having trouble expressing himself. I was thunderstruck that they did not see the beauty in his descriptions, and I told them that they did not appreciate his unique ability to express himself. They were critical of my explanations, and one felt that I was denying that Joshua had a problem. She pointed out that when some-one asked Joshua a point-blank question, he would draw a total blank. This, she said, was very disturbing.

Listening to Joshua's teacher describe his word retrieval difficulties evoked overwhelming feelings in me. I remem-bered the terror that I had felt as a child when I could not remember my mother's or father's name. Sometimes I still freeze when trying to introduce my wife. But Ellen had dealt with that problem intuitively long ago. She has found crea-tive ways to get introduced without involving me. Her as-sumption was that I would never introduce her, so she made arrangements on her own. We both realized that she did this and, though we had never actually spoken about it, we both knew it was an enormous relief to me.

Remembering how ashamed and embarrassed I was as a child, I was especially careful not to make a big deal of the fact that Joshua could not remember certain words or facts. I did not want him to feel upset with himself if he could not remember my name.

I recalled my own struggles with memory, or what some would call selective memory. I could remember a patient's blood test fifteen years later, but found it almost impossible to remember my keys. I have at least five sets of keys because I usually lose about three or four sets per year. I also lose beepers. I am always leaving my telephone somewhere. Di-rections literally go in one ear and out the other. Stethoscopes, wallets, and other items would be with me one minute and gone the next. I assumed that, like me, when Joshua found something he wanted to remember, he would.

I shared my thoughts with Joshua's teachers, but they felt a kindergarten boy should be able to recall his father's name, learn the days of the week, and address a teacher appropriately. They felt that my unusual explanations were a form of denial and that I had difficulty accepting that Joshua had problems. On the other hand, I felt that they were the problem. I felt that Joshua, like myself, would be fine if the teachers were more patient and understanding.

A strange thing was happening. As I was becoming increasingly irritable and combative with the teachers, I was starting to feel great. It struck me that I was doing something for Joshua that no one had ever done for me. My parents had never defended me. When my teachers described the "litany of uns," my parents listened respectfully and accepted their judgment. My parents would get upset and angry and take it out on me. So when Joshua's teachers spoke to us about things that Joshua could not do, I was careful not to get angry with him. I wanted to preserve his happiness.

Unfortunately, while I was thrilled with my insights, Ellen was not. She found my explanations unusual, but more importantly she was worried about what she considered my obsessive comparisons between Joshua and myself. The teachers added fuel to that fire. They told her that that I was making excuses for Joshua and that the comparisons were far-fetched at the very least.

Context and logic were the next issues to come up. Joshua's teachers felt that he did not make sense because his thoughts were out of order, or seemed totally irrelevant. He also did not seem to be able to follow a conversation. They called these problems organizational or processing issues, which are perceived as a type of learning disability, and recommended further evaluations and tutoring. But we had already been through that the previous year and it was not helpful. I explained to them that I disagreed with their evaluation. I understood that he needed to make himself understood to the rest of the world, and I felt if they gave him more time and probed his answers a little more they would see. I explained that we had developed a certain type of patter over the years. We did not actually have single conversations so much as multiple, parallel, long, never-ending stream of consciousness talks. It suited Joshua and me. When Joshua said something, I automatically stored it, realizing that he might come back to it at any time or place. I simply went on with my business and pieced his thoughts together at some later date if it was possible. The order that things came out or how long it took did not matter that much to me. I knew what he meant.

I realized that Joshua said things that seemed out of context, but I assumed that was because he had so many thoughts banging around in his brain and that he was not yet able to control their flow. While this made it difficult to understand him, sometimes it also allowed for unusual links to form among the things that were still stuck inside his head. My perception was that Joshua's thoughts always had context if you could just step back to allow a broader perspective.

Joshua's teachers were becoming increasingly frustrated with his inability to do things in class and with what they perceived as my inability to accept that reality. They found a more sympathetic and accepting audience in Ellen. Poor Ellen was caught in the middle. She had never known any school problems, so she had no experience in how to deal with the issue. There was a general agreement among the teachers and experts that there was something wrong with our boy. When we were alone I was always able to convince Ellen of my beliefs. But when she would speak with a teacher, she returned with doubts.

I had always prided myself on my logic, and I forced myself to look deep within myself to sort out and understand my feelings. I knew I had to distance myself from any thoughts about resemblances in thinking, learning, and verbalization between Joshua and me. I challenged myself to see if it were possible that he had significant problems that I was refusing to see. But since this was as much about love as intellect, I looked into my heart first for clues.

There had been a series of recent conversations that specifically stood out. While I understood that Joshua could often be exasperating and go off in many different directions, seemingly unable to focus on only one, there was a recent experience where he seemed to have a hyperfocus.

Joshua and I had nightly conversations, and I was comfortable talking about most anything. There was one topic, however, that I had never discussed with anyone before: my father. I hadn't cried for him, and I didn't talk about him. The subject was too upsetting and confusing. My father was a relatively young man when he died suddenly and unexpectedly of a heart attack. In the sudden death of a seemingly healthy person, there is no time to understand and accept, no time to make peace. This was exactly how it was with my father. Joshua wanted to talk about him, and had an insatiable desire to know more. Many nights he would ask "Could you tell me a story about 'that man when you were a boy?' " At first I was somewhat hesitant, but he badgered me relentlessly, eager for some understanding of the relationship my father and I had. For some reason he needed to talk about it. The first thing I told him was that my father had been the only person who ever called me Brucie. Joshua was thrilled with this tidbit of information. He checked it with my mother just to make sure I was telling the truth. When she confirmed the nickname, it only whetted his appetite for more information.

One burning issue for Joshua was tickling. Joshua was unbelievably ticklish, and he loved being tickled. I would tickle him for hours and he never tired of it. Therefore, he wanted to know, in detail, the tickling history of my daddy and me. I explained to him that I couldn't really remember my father tickling me, though I remembered that when he came home from work he would sit down on a large blue easy chair in the living room and I would tickle him on the back of his neck. As I told Joshua the story I remembered how much fun it was. It gave me a good feeling just to talk about it. Suddenly Joshua began furiously jumping up and down on the bed, and acting like he had just heard the most interesting and important news of his life. Then he started to tickle me behind my neck. I had visions of tickling my father like it was yesterday, except that I saw myself as my father and Joshua as me. He tickled and tickled and tickled. Unlike my father, but exactly like Joshua, I was very ticklish. I laughed so hard my sides hurt and I thought I was going to cry. As he tickled I felt suddenly unburdened, as if a tremendous weight floated up and off my shoulders. Joshua had searched for and found a link between my father and me and him: tickling on the neck.

Joshua's questions were not eloquently presented. Yet his relentless searching, incisive probing, and sensitivity were, to me, remarkable for such a young child. Joshua's teachers were telling me that he was confused, disorganized, inattentive, and badly behaved, but I felt there was a body of evidence that pointed to a different, but not significantly impaired, child. I was convinced I was right about him.

Ellen was becoming more vocal about the fact that she

did not like my attitude with the teachers. She felt I was being dismissive of their concerns. I felt that they were being dismissive of my experience as a doctor and my intuition as a parent. We both knew there was a major storm brewing.

Joshua's classroom behavior was more of an immediate problem to his teachers than anything else. They felt that he was a disruptive influence in the class. Joshua was unable to sit still, unable to stand in line, unable to pay attention, unable to control his impulse to speak out at inappropriate times, and unable to generally control his boundless energy. We had noticed this as well.

Neither Joshua nor I could sit still for very long. For instance, when we went to a restaurant we would order our food and immediately bolt from the table to wait outside the restaurant until our food arrived. We would throw a ball, play tag, and have races. Joshua would periodically run in to check on the status of our order. Whenever possible we would search for a restaurant that had windows where we could just look in so as not to bother the other patrons. I knew that this was rude and I always felt bad about abandoning Ellen and Aaron. But Aaron could sit still. For Joshua and me, a quick escape and physical activity were the only remedies for our restlessness.

While I did not mind Joshua's activity level, I realized that it could be distracting in a classroom. The teachers spoke to Ellen and me about this. They were concerned that Joshua's hyperactivity was increasingly becoming a problem for the entire class. I assured the teachers that I would speak to Joshua and asked them what I could specifically talk to him about.

Joshua was having trouble playing games with the other children, they said. This at first astonished us. Joshua loved to play. Yet they were very clear that when it came to simple board games he seemed unteachable. He would move his pieces the wrong number of spaces, or in the wrong direction, and often confused his piece with those of the other children. He would move the other players' pieces on purpose when they weren't looking, and by mistake when they were. He was fidgety and restless, occasionally knocking over the board and ruining the game for everyone.

I could understand how disruptive Joshua's game playing could be in the classroom, but I could also understand Joshua's point of view. I had always hated board games. I often upended the game board, relieved at ending it, although I realized it often upset the other players. The rules of games always confounded me.

Again Ellen reminded me that we were talking about Joshua, not me, but I was finding the distinction between my and Joshua's behavior more difficult to discern each time something like this would come up. I assured the teachers that I could and would take care of it. I began playing board games with Joshua every day after school in an effort to not only teach him, but to understand why the teachers thought he was unteachable.

I chose Parcheesi. I never liked it, but I was determined

to stick with it for Joshua's benefit. It turned out to be an enlightening and enjoyable experience for me even though the way we played might have seemed odd. I noticed that when Joshua cheated, it was more out of frustration than cunning. He could not count spaces, understand what to do next, or even recognize which piece was his. He knew he wanted to win but was having trouble figuring out how. He cheated because it was the only way he could figure out how to play the game. I spent long hours with him, teaching him how to recognize his pieces and how to count the spaces, and to be careful not to knock over the board. I also reinforced that he could not cheat under any circumstance at school. I told him he could cheat when he played with me, just for fun, but not at school. It was a difficult lesson for him to learn, but he could soon play board games.

I was not remotely concerned about Joshua's intellect. He was an absolute delight to play with—we laughed a lot, he was learning how to play games, and it was a great bonding experience. We both felt liberated by not feeling constrained by the rules, or worrying about upsetting the other when the board upended, as it invariably did. Ellen soon found it a lot easier to play games with Joshua and things seemed to be going along well, as it was now obvious to Ellen and me that I could teach Joshua things that his teachers could not. This distressed me because I wasn't employing any brilliant techniques; I was simply using repetition, kindness, and fun.

Joshua's teachers were also concerned about his eating habits and felt that we should be sending Joshua to school with a better lunch than just bread and water. Ellen explained that Joshua would only eat plain whole-wheat bread and drink bottled water. We tried to get him to eat other things but he wouldn't. In fact, when we tried he would simply vomit.

Ellen and I had tried everything we could think of but Joshua did not like any food except for bread and water. Every morning he would grudgingly eat hot oatmeal. For lunch, he would have bread and water. For dinner, bread and water. He did not like or eat vegetables, fruits, meat, chicken, pasta, or rice, though he would occasionally eat a half a hot dog or chicken nuggets at McDonald's. I had considered the possibility that food could in some way be related to behavior, and had been very careful not to give Joshua junk food. In fact, until the age of four, he had never had a piece of cake or a cookie and had never tasted candy, ice cream, or soda. I was proud of that although as I explained it to the teachers I could sense their disapproval. I was being perceived as an overbearing, rigid parent heartlessly denying his little child some sweets.

I had seen kids with eating habits like Joshua's in my practice. It was very upsetting to the parents, but I had always counseled them to keep offering different foods but not make too big a deal of it. When kids were ready they would eat. Joshua was skinny, but no more than other children his age that ate well, so we did not make a major issue out of it. I expressed this to his teachers but they didn't seem to believe me.

By that time Ellen was very concerned about the teachers' complaints about Joshua's behavior, learning, and speech. She still wasn't quite sure what to think about the testing from last year. We weren't speaking much because every conversation ended up with me trying to convince her that Joshua would be okay or that I should home school him, or we would argue about the teachers, testers, and experts. But the way I taught Joshua to play games made a point. I sensed a slight change in Ellen's attitude. I was starting to pull her, ever so slightly, to my side. After all, the teachers had told her Joshua could not learn to play games and they were wrong about that. That planted a little seed of doubt in her mind about the teachers and brought me a tiny bit of credibility. We both sensed the slight change of momentum but we did not discuss it. Both of us were watching Joshua a little more critically. We were now noticing Joshua's difficulties in other areas that we could not ever have imagined.

Kindergarten is when kids start to play team sports such as soccer, baseball, and basketball, and it is when Little League generally begins. Joshua was deliriously happy just thinking about it. He loved anything that was active and we were hoping he could taste some success in sports to balance the constant disapproval he was getting in school. We were ready for some good news, and for activities that might tire Joshua out.

The first team sport that Joshua played was soccer. I was vigilant in looking for any troubling patterns. There were a few small things that I noticed but in general all went well.

The coach explained the need for warming up and showed them how to do some exercises. Joshua listened intently and did the exercises, but when they got to jumping jacks he faded away. At first this did not seem especially significant, but as the season progressed it was apparent to everyone that Joshua would not do the exercises. I could not understand why: He always seemed to enjoy anything physical. Joshua would not talk to me about it so I thought I would give him some space until I could find out what the problem was. In any case, one thing was certain. Wherever the ball was, Joshua was the first person to get to it. He made some breathtaking moves on the field. He also spent time talking to some of the opposing players during the game or staring at his shoes or sometimes just looking up in the air. A few times he walked off the field to tell me he was thirsty without any apparent concern or understanding that a game was going on. I took to standing on the sideline and shouting instructions such as "Wake up," "Stop looking at your shoes," or "Kick the ball." I was very careful not to make it seem like I was yelling at him, but rather coaching or rooting, and I would never be negative. In the beginning it was clear that Joshua could not function without my help, but as the season progressed he needed less and less of my personal coaching.

The next sport he participated in was basketball, which is a very different game from soccer. The playing area is smaller, the game quicker, and it requires intense focus and determination. It was immediately clear that Joshua was confused. He could dribble and shoot, which was more than most of the five-year-olds could do, but he had trouble keeping track of what else he was supposed to do. One day he was playing a game on a court and there was a loose ball in a game on the neighboring court. Joshua took off and ran for the ball and started dribbling. Suddenly he stopped. I shouted, and when he saw me he dropped the ball and came over. He had seen a flash of the ball and he ran for it, forgetting about the game he was in. From then on, I prowled the sidelines like a hawk. I was his personal coach, telling him where to run, and what to do.

I enjoyed helping the kids play basketball because I love kids and I would have enjoyed teaching them anything. At first I didn't know much about it, but I bought quite a few books on the subject so that I could be a better coach. I became the non-coach coach for kids with problems. I found that there were similarities between these kids and Joshua. They were all struggling to play the game. But Joshua's problem was unique. He found it difficult to remember which hoop was his, what number he was, who he was supposed to cover, or even which basketball court he should be on. With my coaching from the sidelines, Joshua was able to function. Once again, as the season progressed he needed less and less help from me.

Having now taught Joshua board games, soccer, and basketball, I was developing an understanding about the way Joshua needed to learn things. He was very different from the other children and he appeared seriously impaired because of the types of things he did not understand. He would often understand the complex and miss the simple. However, once the obvious was pointed out to him he could function. I was hoping the teachers would do this for him, but if they couldn't, I would.

The complaints from Joshua's school increased. The teachers wanted to speak to Ellen or me almost every single day about something that Joshua was unable to do. They seemed to be constantly assailing us with what they perceived as our parental imperfections: that I did not want to accept the reality of an impaired son, and that Ellen waffled on the issues. Then, of course, there was the "Lunch Problem." Repeatedly we explained Joshua's eating issues. They insisted that we were in denial, and we felt the same about them. Everything, it now seemed, was adversarial.

I remembered my mother's story about how the teachers would lie in wait for her on parent-teacher night. "Mrs. Roseman, I want to speak with you," they'd say. Now that I was a doctor, my mother delighted in retelling this story, pointing out how far I had come. I knew that she was proud of me but now I was realizing for the first time how painful that particular memory was for me. I was getting flashes of how I had felt at that time. I realized that my teachers were angry with me and that my mother was angry with me for what the teachers said. My father was angry about what my mother told him and my brothers were angry about how angry everybody was because of me. I was the object of everyone's anger. I was ashamed and humiliated by it all.

Just as I did not like it when my mother told my story, I did not like it when, Joshua's teachers spoke to me like that about Joshua. It evoked those old feelings of shame and humiliation about my abilities, and accounted for my resentment at teachers for causing it. I didn't want my son to suffer as I had. I thought Joshua was a delightful, wonderful child and I simply refused to allow them to say things about him that I thought were unfair. No one could make me feel ashamed of my boy. To me he was the greatest.

The "litany of uns" was now in full force and I decided I needed a better understanding of the nature of all the problems Joshua was having. I asked for and received permission to audit some of Joshua's classes. I noticed things that were extremely upsetting to me—not to Joshua or his teachers, just to me. Most disturbing to me was that Joshua was becoming increasingly excluded from class activities; he was becoming marginalized. One day as I was observing the cooking activity, I became worried by the way Joshua was reacting to the teacher's attitude. All the kids would measure ingredients and make something. Joshua clearly had a hard time with this. Instead of helping him, the teachers tried to ignore him. Joshua was getting used to being ignored. However, he was appreciative of what little time the teachers spent with him. He did not ask questions when he did not understand something, and I could see that the children who understood quickly became a separate class within the class. Joshua clearly recognized that he was not included in the inner class, and his body wriggled and moved as he struggled to hold in his questions. When the teachers finally did get around to him it was as if they were allowing a beggar boy to pick up the pieces of food that had fallen from the table. To him it was feast, and he luxuriated in the attention, but more often than not he could not remember his questions and did not get any scraps of help from them.

Joshua was not the only child I observed as I evaluated the dynamics of the class. It was clear that the teachers had favorites who always were given the benefit of the doubt. It was also clear that certain children were blamed for things they didn't do or mean. I noticed that Joshua, like these other out-of-favor kids, gravitated toward the back of the room. I remembered my own "last row" syndrome. But the most important thing that I noticed—and which deeply disturbed me—was that the teachers spent more time with the children who needed the least help. This was diametrically opposed to how I thought it should be.

It upset me that when I confronted the teachers with my opinions they accused me of being in denial about my son's problems. They felt that they gave him easier tasks because he could not do the more difficult ones. I felt that he could do what was required if he was given a little more time. It came down to a major difference of emphasis and respon-sibility: I felt they had teaching disabilities and they felt I had parenting disabilities. So once again, I noted what Joshua could not do and resolved to teach it to him myself. I began to teach him to cook. We started making chocolate pudding and I helped him measure, and I let him break eggs.

Once again he was learning and I was employing methods of repetition, kindness, and fun.

On another occasion Ellen and I were both able to observe something that helped put Joshua's situation in perspective for us. The students sat on a large rug encircling the head teacher. Joshua was the only child seated on a chair. The assistant teachers glared at him from either side of the room, and then looked at each other, rolled their eyes, and shrugged in unison. They then looked toward us with a forced half-smile betraying their true feelings. Within seconds, Joshua went from sitting erect on his chair seat to balancing himself on the seat on his belly and parallel to the floor, then falling down and scrambling back noisily to his original position. Variations on this theme were repeated endlessly at a dizzying rate. I had seen this routine before; it was reminiscent of my own childhood. I found it amusing and endearing. I could see the teachers were annoyed by Joshua's level of activity by the way they kept glancing at him. I realized that this could be unsettling to the class, but it did not appear to bother any of the other kids. I knew that he had to stop that behavior, but I wasn't quite sure how. I knew that punishing him was not the answer. It had been tried on me and it never worked.

The head teacher scanned the semicircle of children and carefully engaged each child's eyes and nodded as she said, "Today we are going to talk about food. Let's go around the room, and everybody say what their favorite food is."

She fixed her gaze on the child to her immediate left and

he stated, softly and confidently, "Ice cream." The rest of the circle nodded in accord. "Very good," said the teacher as she directed her gaze toward the next child. He said ice cream, too, as did the next four or five kids until one brave and confidant child switched to pizza. This time the other children aggressively nodded in agreement and the teacher said, "Excellent." One kid said carrots and everybody had a good laugh over that, although the carrot kid was obviously embarrassed. The teacher did not seem to mind that many kids repeated the same answer. In fact, it made perfect sense. The previous kid had already observed the reactions of the class *and* the teacher, so he or she knew what to expect. No one was going to say carrots again, that was for sure. If the other kids laughed or the teacher frowned, you would avoid that answer like poison. If the other kids nodded in agreement and the teacher was pleased, you knew it was safe to proceed. It was clear that pizza was a good response. The kids nodded and the teacher smiled.

I tensed when it was Joshua's turn. Although the question seemed ridiculously simple, I knew it was a *tough* one for Joshua. He did not *like* food and didn't know much about it.

"And what is your favorite food, Joshua?" the teacher asked.

Joshua didn't respond.

"Joshua Roseman," the teacher said, speaking louder and more slowly, "What is your favorite food?"

"I love my uncle Jeffrey . . ." he began.

The teacher cut Joshua off, and with the moment punctuated by a smattering of giggles, moved on. It was clear that she did not feel that Joshua's answer merited further exploration. It stood in stark contrast to the other more "appropriate" answers, like pizza, ice cream, and even carrots, all of which she had taken the time to discuss. No, Joshua had given the wrong answer to the question; the kids knew it, and the teacher knew it, and as she unceremoniously moved on, Joshua hung his head.

Joshua had given what appeared to be an inappropriate answer to a straightforward question. But I knew that Joshua understood the question because his answer made perfect sense to me. He simply expressed himself in a way that his teachers did not understand. His answer was as endearing as it was brilliant. It was the very essence of what he was. Joshua loved his uncle Jeffrey, fiercely. Jeffrey had recently made him an apple cake in an effort to get him to enlarge his food repertoire. Joshua was thrilled by Jeffrey's stories of how my mother had made the cake for my brothers and me and how much we had all loved it. The fact I had never liked that cake as a child made no difference. Joshua tasted the cake because his uncle Jeffrey had baked it especially for him. Joshua knew that his uncle Jeffrey was a good cook and he loved listening as Jeffrey regaled him with stories about parties he threw, and what he cooked. Joshua didn't understand what Jeffrey was saying, but he loved listening to it anyway. Joshua wanted to be part of the life of his beloved uncle Jeffrey. So what was Joshua's favorite food? It was anything that allowed him to be immersed in an ocean of love for his uncle Jeffrey. Whatever food uncle Jeffrey made for him was Joshua's favorite food.

Pizza could be discussed—crust, cheese, sauce—but "I love my uncle Jeffrey" made no sense at all. To the teachers it seemed clear that Joshua was not paying attention or did not understand the question or could not or would not think of an appropriate answer. But Joshua *was* thinking. He was thinking in a way that no other child in that class was. He was making a creative effort to understand what his favorite food was and struggling to understand why. But to his teachers Joshua Roseman was the kid who *always* had the *wrong answer*. Just like his father before him.

I knew then that I was in thrall to overpowering emotions, and there was not necessarily anything I could do about it. My training as a doctor was suddenly pushed aside as painful memories flooded over me. Something gripped my chest and began to squeeze. Trying desperately to maintain my composure, I barely found the strength to control my emotions. I realized at that moment that though I had borne my own pain and suffering, I could not bear the heartache of watching my son suffer the wounds from those same painful arrows. Unlike the first time, I was now prepared and I could do something about it. I could use my intellect, determination, and medical expertise to go back in time to treat myself, and the benefit would go to my son. It was a powerful and wonderful thought.

It was at about the same time that Joshua began wearing a baseball cap. He had a collection of them and was always asking for more. Soon he would not leave the house without it. He pushed the brim down over his face so we could hardly see him. We didn't know what this was about, but it was worrisome to the teachers and Ellen and even I thought it strange. Although we were perplexed it did not seem like a big deal. I remembered my mother always complaining about not being able to see my face, so I tried not to bother Joshua too much about it. It did occur to me, though, that maybe Joshua was hiding.

Keeping up with the "litany of uns" from the teachers was impossible. Ellen and I were becoming frustrated. Though she agreed that I had some success at teaching him certain skills, we were arguing about how to best deal with Joshua. All of the air was being sucked out of the house.

Each night Ellen and I made phone calls to parents who we had heard about with similar problems and asked what, if anything, they had learned. I made professional inquiries. It was terribly frustrating. There seemed to be a lot of parents around in a lot of different schools who were having problems with their kids. The parents of children in public schools assumed that if their child was in private school, that would be the answer. The private school parents considered switching schools. But there did not seem to be one place that everybody thought was good. Everyone agreed about only one thing: No school seemed to be able to deal with kids like Joshua who did not fit the mold. I was beginning to think that Joshua needed to be in a special school for children with problems, and I gave more serious thought to home schooling. We knew that we would have to do something drastic before the following year.

Ever more ominous signs were beginning to appear. Joshua was accepting that there was something wrong with him. The teachers did not bother to teach him because he was harder to teach. The result was that he made less of an attempt to learn. It was a self-fulfilling prophecy. His self-esteem was getting lower and lower, he was learning less and less, and he was blaming himself. The teachers felt vindicated. The brim of his hat was getting lower and it was now impossible to get him to take it off. He even wanted to sleep in it.

The situation was getting very tense. To school officials I was an overprotective, incredibly bad-humored parent, angry about having a learning disabled son and refusing to accept the situation. They considered my demands unreasonable, and thought I was unfairly blaming the teachers. Their disdain for my son was clear. They kept insisting that I accept my son for what he was. At a meeting with the ECD, the suggestion of psychotherapy came up. To them the problems were Learning Disabilities and parental disabilities, both of which foisted the blame onto Joshua or me and Ellen, and away from them and their methods. They reminded me repeatedly that Joshua's evaluation from the preceding year had predicted these problems. I responded by pointing out that, like the expert, they did not know what they were talking about. Nobody appreciated comments like that from me, but I no longer cared.

Our home became just like my house when I was a kid: same script, different actors. The teachers did not like Joshua, Ellen and I were arguing, and Aaron cowered in his room when anything was said that upset him—and all this conflict about Joshua invariably upset him. My patients were even beginning to ask me if anything was wrong, which concerned me. I felt that I looked the same and did not feel that my performance was suffering. The patients agreed, but they said there was a sense of sadness about me. I was touched that so many patients cared enough to mention it, but I was also worried about it.

I wasn't getting along with my wife, my patients were worried about me, and I was constantly fighting with Joshua's teachers. I realized that my life was falling apart, but I was so convinced that I was correct about Joshua and so worried about what would happen to him if I did not intercede that I remained steadfast. I told Ellen that I would have to redouble my efforts. Then things got worse.

Once again we found ourselves in a meeting with the ECD. She felt that things were simply getting out of hand and she thought that a meeting with all the involved parties and the Learning Specialist was in order. Ellen and I agreed.

We braced ourselves for the worst. The teachers spoke to us about a problem different from any we had thus far encountered: Kindergarten was almost over, and Joshua was almost six years old, but he could not count to five, nor could he learn the alphabet.

After having rejected the teachers' assertions about

Joshua's inability to learn, his attitude, his behavior, and his speech, my worst fear became a reality. Joshua, almost 6 years old could not count past three, and I was unable to teach him how to do it. For the first time I felt that there was something that I could not teach him. I had worked with him in my usual way with repetition, fun, and kindness, but I was stuck. There was nothing I could do. Joshua also could not learn the alphabet. I would go over letter books with him and it seemed to me that he recognized his letters, but he could not learn to say the alphabet. I was becoming frantic. I realized that learning the alphabet was very different than not knowing the names of days. I could understand his problems with days because the concept had always eluded me too: Days, nights, weekends, holidays, are all the same to me. But without the alphabet, he would not be able to learn to read.

I went to bookstores and searched the web once again, seeking books and data on developmental milestones. There were many popular books that defined "What your child should know" in each grade, or age and so on. I pored over these books to see if it was really important that Joshua be able to master the alphabet and counting. Remembering the children in my practice I realized that I had never had one who could not count to five while in kindergarten. I began looking around at other people's children to see if I could find one child of Joshua's age who could not count to five. I tried counting with him all the time to see if he could remember just up to five. He couldn't. I was beside myself with worry. For the first time, as they explained about Joshua's problems with the alphabet and counting, I had no answer. I knew that Joshua knew the sounds of his letters but I could not even bring myself to point this out.

Our appointment with the Learning Specialist was interesting. She, like the expert, was late, but she darted quickly, key in hand and artfully aimed at the lock as she flicked her neck and motioned us in. The office was spartan, a windowless, airless, room, barely large enough to hold three chairs. She sat down on the largest chair and swiveled around to look at us as we sat down on the children's school chairs.

She talked about personal matters, regaling us with stories of her professional life, and told us about her daughter, who had learning disabilities and who was now at an elite college. She explained that she had spoken to Joshua's teachers and that she understood the situation. She told us in no uncertain terms that she believed that Joshua had severe learning disabilities. He had warning signs that indicated he would have future difficulties in school. She felt that Joshua should have speech therapy in spite of what we felt, and said that he needed daily tutoring. She said that she would be testing him personally very soon to evaluate the situation with his numbers and letters. She said the teachers had mentioned that I no longer observed his classes and made demands, and she was happy about that. I made no attempt to explain that I stopped because I had given up on the teachers listening to anything that I had to say. She said she would speak with the teachers in an attempt to defuse the emotionally charged atmosphere. We felt relatively good after the meeting although we had no illusions.

Over the next few weeks and as the school year was concluding, we took stock of Joshua's situation. His stammering suddenly became much less frequent, though it could still be severe. He played games well without cheating. His teachers felt that his behavior also had improved, though I suspected that they were simply ignoring him, not that he was better behaved. I was thinking about other alternatives to his current school, such as a school for children with special needs or home schooling where at least, I reasoned, I would not have to fight with any teachers and other school personnel. I had given up on the teachers, just like they had given up on Joshua, and Joshua had given up on himself. But I had not given up on Joshua and he had not given up on me.

The final parent-teacher conference for kindergarten arrived. The head teacher sat flanked by the other teachers. She had a large page of notes, and it was clear that she was the designated speaker. She began to tell us about Joshua. She felt he had learning disabilities, had a behavior problem, was disorganized, and rarely had any idea what was going on in class. Most important, he could not count or learn the alphabet and she felt he should be left back.

I mentioned that I had begun to teach Joshua to read on my own. I was making some progress, and that had made me feel a little better about the fact that Joshua could not count past three. She explained that it was not a good idea for a parent teach his or her own child to read because ultimately the child would resent the parent. The danger was that the child would end up not liking to read and not liking the parent, and so it should be left to professionals. We were stunned, to say the least. I did not feel that any first-year teacher, even with an Ivy League masters degree, was in a position to state so categorically that everything that I was saying and doing was wrong. We left the meeting, Ellen in tears and me angry. We then had a quickly arranged meeting with the Learning Specialist. Ms. Masters Degree was there. So was the ECD. The Learning Specialist began. She had personally tested Joshua, observed him in class, and spoken with him. She was concerned about Joshua's inability to count to five or learn to recognize his letters. She said that this was an important indicator of a child's future ability to read and succeed. She did not feel that leaving Joshua back would help, he would just have the same problems the next year.

Ellen and I were stunned. We had been prepared for the fact that Joshua would be left back, but we were shocked to find that the Learning Specialist was much more pessimistic than we could have imagined. What did she mean by saying that leaving him back would not even help? Was she confirming what the expert had told us about a pervasive developmental disorder? My mind was racing, and I did not know what to say.

Ellen had an interesting question. Joshua had mentioned to her that when the Learning Specialist tested him she was very tired and kept yawning. Ellen was curious what that meant.

As the Learning Specialist began to go through the file with Joshua's test, she explained some of the questions and Joshua's shortcomings to us. For instance, she had asked him to give her word that began with *ah* (the letter a). This was a test to see if he understood that a letter had a certain sound. He didn't.

My wife broke in and said, "No, he said that you yawned five times in a row, which he showed by holding up five fingers on one hand."

As the Learning Specialist read to us the exact way she had phrased the question, we all suddenly understood what had happened. She had said, "Give me another word that begins with *ah*, do you know a word that begins with *ah*, *ah* is a sound, do you know any words with it," and so on? She had asked Joshua the same question in five different ways. Every time she said the word *ah* he obviously thought she was yawning. It was clear that he did not understand the question. While we realized that this was a definite problem, it was certainly not what the Learning Specialist believed, which was that Joshua did not know his letters.

I pointed out to her that I had been teaching Joshua to read in an unusual but effective manner using phonemes (letter groups) and that he was reading very slightly. "That is impossible," she said. I explained that he read for me every night. He could read best at around 9 P.M.

She said, "He cannot read in school. He cannot read for me."

I said, "Well he can read for me."

She said, "If he can't read for me, he can't read."

Unlike that little first-grade boy, paralyzed as the awful truth penetrated his psyche, I responded decisively, "Well if he can read for me, he *can* read."

It was clear that everyone was uncomfortable as I reverted to my old combative self. We needed to move on. I had an idea that I believed was cost effective and, as a last ditch effort, was worth a trial. Ritalin has been prescribed for many children with hyperactivity and/or ADD, so I suggested that we simply try Ritalin for two weeks to see if it helped. I was shocked at the response to what I considered a suggestion that would lead to simply gaining additional insight into what might work for Joshua.

"You are always making excuses for your son's problems and are looking for the answers in a bottle and we cannot allow that." She also said that she considered my suggestion a form of "child abuse." I was struck dumb. I work with patients on Ritalin and I thought that my suggestions should have been considered. Moreover my office was four blocks from the school. Such an accusation could have destroyed my reputation and my ability to earn a living, not to mention hurt my feelings. Faced with that shocking accusation, I was suddenly in a position of defending myself in addition to

Joshua. I worked quickly, utilizing connections, influence, and money. How, I wondered, could other people without these resources even begin to cope with a situation like this?

Within hours I had arranged for Joshua, Ellen, and I to be evaluated by three very highly regarded psychiatrists over the next five days. From the outset we felt comfortable with all three. First we saw Dr. Stanley Turecki, Physician-in-charge of Beth Israel Hospital's Difficult Child Center and author of two bestselling and important books, *The Difficult Child* and *Normal Children Have Problems Too*. I knew him professionally, having referred patients to him and having occasionally sought his counsel on difficult patients. I was always impressed with his insight, knowledge, and kindness. He had an unusual but effective lead in. After interviewing Joshua he asked Joshua if he wanted to jump up and down on his couch. Joshua could barely believe his good fortune and as he approached the couch he kept looking back at me, Ellen, and Dr. Turecki for reassurance that it was okay. We all nodded, and Dr. Turecki even gave him a few words of encouragement. Ellen and I nodded, and a moment later Joshua jumped on the couch and exploded with enough energy to heat Canada. He was springing up and down on the couch, really taking it to the cushions. When he was finished, the ice had been broken. Joshua thought Dr. Turecki was the greatest and wanted to know when he could come back again. Ellen and I were also put at ease by the display. It was easier to talk about our boy. And we did.

The next psychiatrist had a different technique. He had

an enormous box of action figures. We knew that they were expensive and were shocked when he gave one to Joshua. Needless to say, Joshua was his friend for life.

The last psychiatrist that we saw was simply a nice man with a calm demeanor. He didn't do anything special but it was easy to feel comfortable in his presence. Ellen and I were amazed at how different these experiences were from what we had recently been through. None of the doctors spoke to us about their private lives. None were interested in me. All of them had forms such as a Connor scale, which is a rating scale to evaluate if a child has ADD and must be filled out by the parents and the teachers. None of them felt the need to do an exhaustive battery of expensive tests. They were all able to do what they had to do in a fraction of the time and at one tenth of the cost of the "expert" we had previously seen. All of the psychiatrists' styles were dramatically different but the substance was essentially the same. They were careful in their collection of data but took few notes. They acted in what I considered to be a professional manner.

We finally decided on Dr. Turecki because we felt most comfortable with him. Additionally, we felt that considering the attitude at Joshua's school, we needed a physician who was beyond reproach. In any case, they all had the same thoughts on diagnosis and treatment:

1. Diagnosis: ADHD, possible learning disabilities.

2. Treatment: two-week trial of Ritalin.

We were comfortable with the way Dr. Turecki handled things. After interviewing Ellen and me for about an hour, he saw Joshua alone. Finally he spoke to all of us together, at which time he laid out a treatment plan: a trial of a stimulant, Ritalin, being the best studied and most often used. Very often one could tell quickly if the medication worked, although the dose might need adjusting.

I felt comfortable that a trial of Ritalin would serve two functions. First, it would help clarify the diagnosis. Second, it would be considered a treatment for Joshua's problems. For instance, if Joshua could learn his letters or count while on the Ritalin, that would tell us that this was a chemical problem and should be treated with medication. If it was a psychological problem, we could send him for therapy. Of course there was the possibility that the problem could be both chemical and psychological.

Ellen was philosophically opposed to the use of medication to control Joshua's behavior or make it easier for him to learn. She did, however, agree to a two-week trial as a diagnostic tool. As Dr. Turecki laid out a treatment plan I realized how comfortable I was in allowing him to direct Joshua's care. It was a relief that the focus had shifted way from me.

Dr. Turecki chose to start Joshua on 2.5 mg of Ritalin and felt it would be best if he started on a Saturday morning for two reasons. One, we could observe him carefully, and two, if Joshua had a side effect it was best that it did not happen in school. The following Saturday we made arrangements for Aaron to be out of the house. In the morning I crushed the small pill in a special pill crusher I had bought. I placed the powder carefully in the middle of an Oreo cookie that I had carefully broken open. As I looked down at the white powder on the white icing I realized that the powder was not even noticeable. I carefully closed the cookie and called Joshua, and to his astonishment told him he could have a cookie for breakfast. I told him there was some medicine in the cookie and he would hardly even taste it.

"What do I need medicine for, I'm not sick?"

"I want to see if it helps you concentrate better."

He was not buying it. On the other hand, he wanted the cookie so he decided to overlook his philosophical considerations and ate the cookie with glee.

Joshua was all dressed. Ellen and I tried to act casual as we talked and tried to stay out of his way. He played with his cars and was his usual energetic self. After about thirty minutes I noticed something odd. He was starting to yawn, and he sat on the couch, relaxing. Joshua never relaxed so we knew something was up. So did he.

I sat on a chair and Ellen sat on the couch and we tried not to stare at him but we really couldn't help it. Joshua looked at us looking at him. He thought it was odd but he was a good sport and just sort of went with the flow. After about forty-five minutes Joshua turned to me and said,

"Daddy, when is my birthday?"

"In twelve days," I answered.

"Hmmmm" said Joshua, "twelve, eleven, ten, nine, eight, seven, six, five, four, three, two, one. That doesn't seem very far away."

Ellen and I sat there, shocked, speechless, and paralyzed. It took at least thirty seconds for me to even get a sound out.

"Can you count to thirty?" I asked.

He started to count and got to twenty-three, skipped twenty-four and said twenty-five, when he caught himself and said, "No, wait a minute, I forgot twenty-four," so he want back and continued on to thirty.

I looked at Ellen, she looked at me, and we both looked at Joshua. We were dumbfounded. Joshua was now yawning repeatedly and appeared drowsy. We just sat there shaking our heads and looking at each other. It was the most unusual thing we had ever seen. We didn't know whether to laugh or cry.

On Monday morning I called Dr. Turecki to tell him about what happened. We were still awestruck.

"Did you videotape it?" he asked.

"No, I was too stunned to move."

"Too bad. It is a classic Ritalin response. It would have been great to have it on film."

He was right, but how many people, when faced with what seems to be a miracle remember to run for the movie camera. Joshua's response to the Ritalin was incredible. At the next appointment Dr. Turecki summed it all up by saying. "Joshua is a very different child on this medicine." Nevertheless, Ellen was opposed to medication. It made Joshua ornery and caused headaches and stomach pains. We realized that medication was not the answer for Joshua. It was, however, an extremely important diagnostic tool.

When we went to our next meeting with the Learning Specialist, Dr. Turecki had already called her, and any talk of child abuse seemed to evaporate. She grudgingly agreed to retest Joshua while he was on the Ritalin. I explained the onset of action to her so that she would to be sure to test him at the proper time.

At our next meeting she presented the new evaluation. Having checked previously, we knew the test had been administered at least three hours after the Ritalin dose, so of course we were not surprised when she said reached the same conclusion as previously. Joshua could not count or recognize his letters. We didn't think that she had purposely tested him at the wrong time, but it did not really matter to us. We knew that he could count while on Ritalin though it did not have much of an effect on his ability to read.

When we got home from the meeting Ellen and I played with Joshua and Aaron and hugged them especially tight, realizing how precious they were. They both knew that we were upset. Joshua knew it was because of school. I remembered how I felt when my parents came home from school and were strangely quiet. I knew my father would eventually lecture me and my mother would wail and wonder what she could possibly have done to deserve a child like me. I remembered how my brothers would watch wide-eyed and angry as a hurricane erupted inside the house. Then weeks passed as the damage was repaired but only partially forgotten. My parents would search for punishments for me, feel sorry for themselves, too hurt and upset to have much patience for my brothers or me. I felt rejected and ashamed and I wasn't even sure what I had done wrong.

But I had an opportunity here. I was not my father and Ellen was not my mother. We put smiles on our faces and we all went out to dinner and tried to pretend that nothing had happened. Joshua's birthday was in a few days and we asked Joshua what he wanted for his birthday, "Cupcakes," he replied, "really nice ones—and get an extra one for Aaron." Aaron liked that idea.

chapter six

Teaching Joshua

"If there is one thing on this earth that I know I can do, one thing for which the world has prepared me, it is to teach my learning disabled son to read." That is exactly what I told Ellen . . . and I believed it.

School officials and the plethora of specialists and experts we had consulted summarily dismissed my idea of father as tutor. They explained that a child with special needs requires specialized help. Parents, they pointed out, do not make good teachers. I understood their point, but the more I thought about it the more I became convinced that I had the tools to teach my son. We did, after all, have the same problems.

I knew that there were some effective strategies employed by schools for the learning disabled, and I considered sending Joshua to one of those schools. But I felt that helping him was part of my destiny. I was still smarting from the painful wounds of my youth but I knew that sparing Joshua the same torments I had experienced would validate my suffering and exorcise my guilt.

I felt guilty about Joshua's problems. Ellen was correct when she said to me, "No one in my family ever had anything like this." She didn't mean to hurt my feelings. She was just struggling with her own sense of guilt about having a child with problems. But I knew that Joshua had gotten these problems from me. Having learned a thing or two along the way, I was determined to break the chain. I knew it would be hard but I drew my strength and determination from the heartache of watching Joshua starting to suffer the same torments of my childhood.

When anyone spoke to me about Joshua's problems, I pointed out that he had the same problems that I had. Yet I felt that it was unfair to say that it was only Joshua and I that had the problems. I felt that some of the blame lay with the school. The school's approach to teaching was rigid and seemed to blame the students when they couldn't learn instead of looking for alternative ways of teaching. Maybe some kids had problems learning, but certainly some teachers had problems teaching and I had never heard teachers referred to as having teaching disabilities or teaching problems. It was always the student who had the disabilities and the problems.

Whether I had a disability, or Joshua did, or the teachers

did didn't really matter. I saw only one course of action: I had to prove that Joshua could learn. The teachers, Learning Specialist, Early Childhood Director, and the experts all insisted that Joshua, unable to learn the alphabet, would have great difficulty learning to read, so I decided to tackle that issue head on. I would teach my son to read. I explained my intentions to Ellen, Joshua's teachers, the Learning Specialist, and the psychiatrist. They were all incredulous. Ellen, however, took it the hardest. She agreed that my perspective based on my own experiences might enable me to help Joshua, but she was disturbed by my total disregard for the advice and conclusions of the teaching and learning experts. She was worried about the pressure I would be placing on Joshua and about my missing work. She spoke with school officials, and while they were not totally dismissive, they pointed out that what I wanted to do sounded a little crazy. They asked her if we were having trouble at home. "Yes," she said, as they nodded knowingly and with compassion.

Of course, we *were* having trouble at home, but our problems centered on a single issue: Joshua's problems at school. In the past year we had been told our child had a pervasive developmental disorder, bad attitude, and bad behavior, that he stuttered, was disorganized, unable to take part in a simple conversation or play simple games, and might never learn to read. That did not include the fact that he could not count or learn the alphabet, and that I had been accused of child abuse. Ellen and I, who had rarely ever had disagreements in the previous ten years, were now suddenly disagreeing and fighting constantly about Joshua's problems: how to approach them, how to treat them, who should treat him, where he should go to school, and so on.

It was eerily reminiscent of my home as a child. Yet to me and Ellen and the rest of the non-school world, Joshua was a delight. He stammered, was a bad game player, occasionally shot a basketball in the wrong hoop, confused up and down and Mommy and Daddy, but he was a kind, gentle, generous soul and was popular with children and adults. I loved him and was proud of him—unlike my parents, who loved me but were certainly not proud of me. The barrage of bad reports from school when I was a student drove a wedge between my father and me, and as a result he never really knew me. We spent most of our time arguing about school. He was shocked, hurt, and confused by having a son who was such a "problem." When the teachers told him that I was inattentive, defiant, and lackadaisical, he could not understand why. His response was to tell me that he was going to give the teachers permission to spank me if I could not behave myself. No one ever did, but the message was clear. He thought I was to blame.

My father loved education. At a young age he woke up in the early hours of the morning and went to work. He worked on a milk truck, loading and delivering to stores, schools, and hospitals. After work he went to school, where he relished every moment. He graduated from high school at the age of fourteen and always lamented the fact he could not have stayed longer. He hated his calloused hands and wearing overalls to work on the truck, so after World War II he took advantage of the GI Bill to become a CPA and then went on to law school. He built a prestigious and successful accounting practice, but he always stayed in touch with his true love—education. He became a college advisor and read books on many different subjects. I remember one particular birthday gift from him: a history book about the United States up to 1850. I remember the look in his eye when he told me that if I finished this one he would get me the next one, which covered 1850 to the present. I had been hoping for a toy or even clothes, but I did not want to hurt his feelings so I just said "Thanks." It was his dream, not mine, to get a history book for a birthday present. I was living out his childhood fantasy of attending school on a full belly, unhampered by the demands of work. Yet it had turned into a nightmare, and I was desperately unhappy. He did not understand how I could not sit still, not pay attention, and not learn to add. Why, he wondered, would anyone have a problem at school?

My mother could not understand, either, but in a different way. She had grown up with a sickly father, as a latchkey child, and assumed that her school difficulties were because of the sadness she had to endure. Like me, she was blamed, but in her case there was a perfectly plausible explanation: Her father was always sick. She still smarted from being left back in the second grade. But my mother had accepted placing the blame for her failures on her father's health. She, like my father, couldn't understand why I did poorly in school.

After all, I did not have any sick parents at home; therefore, I had no plausible explanation for not doing well.

My parents thought that I should have been thrilled to be in school unencumbered by hunger, sick parents or work. They were supportive, nurturing, and loving—and heartbroken. Why, they kept asking, couldn't I behave myself at school? Why couldn't I listen more carefully, or stay in my seat, or work harder? Why were they presented with a "litany of uns" at every parent-teacher conference? I could not figure it out either. I wasn't doing anything on purpose, and I didn't understand why everybody was mad at me.

Ultimately, though, my parents' love and my own stubborn determination gave me the strength to overcome the feeling that I was nothing but a problem. It gave me the strength to fight. But the truth is that I was born to fight. From early childhood on, I was a tough guy. If I was pushed, I pushed back. If the teachers picked on me, I found a way to exact my revenge. The more they yelled at me, the more defiant I became.

So far, Joshua had managed to maintain his easygoing nature, but I was worried that he would be forever changed by his school experiences. I did not want the barrage of bad reports from school to drive a wedge between us, as it had between my father and me. I did not want it to totally overwhelm his family life as it had mine. Unfortunately, it had all started to happen anyway.

In searching for ways to help Joshua I thought about my own education. I always needed a little more time to do things, and my class could not wait for me. I remembered struggling to finish tests, and the anxiety I felt when I heard "Time is up, pencils down." I was ashamed because I was slower than the rest of the kids and did not understand things the way they did. The kids in the front rows seemed to possess some special magic that allowed them to finish their tests on time, sit still, and not daydream or look out the window. They knew the answers to the teachers' questions. I wondered how they did it.

Soon my shame turned to anger as the teachers told my parents that if I would only pay better attention or study harder I would do better. I got caught pulling a fire alarm and was brought home by a local policeman. Next I destroyed a large plate glass window with a hammer for no particular reason. The list went on, and soon I was not just bad in school, I was just bad. I did not want that to happen to Joshua.

In observing Joshua's class I realized that very little had changed. The teachers were still in a rush. They spent the most time with the students who needed it the least and the least time with the students who needed it the most. The front rowers got the attention and positive reinforcement and the kids in the back row didn't get the help they needed. Joshua was being shortchanged because the teachers assumed that he could not learn.

I loved to learn and I was good at it. If Joshua had inherited his disabilities/abilities from me, I thought, he should be able to learn, though I was now realizing that it would not be in the way his current teachers were trying to teach him. I did not think that it was he who was the problem. From that moment, whenever I tried to teach Joshua something I began apologizing to him if he had trouble understanding it. I explained that I wasn't a good enough teacher yet and I told him not to worry because I was going to try harder. He always said "Don't worry, Mommy . . . I mean Daddy."

I needed to spend more time discovering novel and interesting ways to teach Joshua. Being a doctor, Joshua's father, and someone who learned differently prepared me for and uniquely qualified me to do this. My medical training had given me an understanding of the scientific method and the need for practice and working long hours in pursuit of a dream. If I could stay up every other night as an intern, I could do it for my son.

I thought about the way the brain worked, and I tried to work from there. When the brain is damaged it tries to find alternate pathways to restore functionality. Joshua's teachers seemed to try to teach him repeatedly by following the same method—without success. I knew that I had to learn to recognize the obstacles, and forge new pathways around them rather than trying the same things over and over again.

I knew that to succeed I needed Joshua's cooperation and fervent commitment. I wasn't sure if such a young child could or would want to help, even if I was doing it for him.

"Joshua, do you understand that you cannot do a lot of the same things as your friends in class?"

He nodded his head yes as he stared at the ground.

"Do you understand that your teachers do not think you can learn to read?" Again the vigorous nod and downward stare, and this time a lowering of the baseball hat brim.

"You and I are the same, Joshua. I can teach you to read."

His head popped up, reminding me of those early mornings peek-ins when he was in his crib. He nodded his head yes and I realized that Joshua Roseman was ready for action—again.

I asked myself, Is it possible that this little boy could possibly understand what I am talking about? After all, he couldn't even count to five. But I understood something that others had seen but not fully appreciated. It was the special relationship that Joshua and I shared. It was what allowed me to be his translator when he was slow to speak. It was what permitted that 5:15 morning mania togetherness. It was the hurt that I understood about how cruel the world could be to people who were different.

Bonded by trust, love, insight, and an obsessive determination, we readied ourselves for a grueling educational adventure. I was ready for the sleepless nights preparing his lessons, and for whatever it took to teach them to him. Joshua was ready, too. I understood that he would do it for me because he loved me, but I also knew that he wanted it for himself, too. He did not like the fact that he could not do what the other kids did in class. Although he accepted and even loved his teachers, he understood that they thought he was dumb. He was not angry like me but he had a fire in his belly just as I did. He wanted to learn and he was thrilled to do it with me. He trusted me and I trusted him. There was never any thought of failure. I was preparing for war, and Joshua . . . well, he was just having fun with his daddy. Luckily neither of us had any idea about the vastness of the task ahead.

To teach Joshua to read, I needed a plan. Syllabi, learning materials, and mentors were not available. This was only about Joshua and me. I would look for answers in his brain by examining and understanding my own. Of course it was pure supposition on my part that we had the exact same neural pathways in our brain. I considered my mother's un-wavering observation that Joshua and I were exactly the same. I also considered that it was a great leap of faith. In reality, though, it came down to one thing. This was an affair of the heart, and ours beat in perfect harmony. I knew that and so did Joshua. I did not know how long that would last, but I decided to trust my heart, and his.

Joshua and I began spending every waking moment questioning and evaluating everything. Ellen resented the time we spent away from her and Aaron. She still worried when Joshua referred to her as Daddy, and that in spite of his good vocabulary he had stammering episodes. She was concerned that the speech therapist was correct about it being a stutter. She was worried that Joshua was often unintelligible to her, and to everyone else but me.

She had another problem: Chasing a boy who moved like the wind and spoke in stammering riddles was exasperating and exhausting. She needed her energy for our other child. Ellen accused me of not spending enough time with Aaron because of my obsession with Joshua. I felt compelled to point out that she seemed more at ease with Aaron and had more patience with him than I had ever seen her show to Joshua. It was an argument with no end. Ellen and I loved and cherished both of our boys, but I knew that I had to work fast because I felt guilty about cheating Aaron. I moved ahead.

chapter seven

Making Sense

I know that a scientific investigation begins with defining the problem and proceeds to hypothesis, theorems, proof, and reproducibility. Being a doctor was a significant asset because I was used to attacking and solving other people's problems. Now it was time to take on one in my own home.

I needed to engage and observe Joshua, and then catalogue the way he interpreted things. Because the senses are the way stimuli from outside or inside the body are received and felt I decided to start there. I remembered from my studies how Aristotle had eloquently described the five senses: sight, hearing, smell, taste, and touch. If I was to understand Joshua's experience of the world, it was logical to start with his senses.

Sight

I was shocked to find that Joshua only saw parts of things. He could look straight at something and miss it completely. For instance, Ellen might say, "Could you pass me the milk?" Joshua could look straight at the milk and say, "I don't see any milk" or she might ask, "Could you hand me that fork?" Joshua would look straight at the fork and say, "What fork?"

How could he not see something that was twelve inches from his face? We had his eyes checked repeatedly, but each time they came back normal.

I am not sure why, but it made sense to me that you could look straight at something and not see it. I had the same problem as a child, and though it had improved as I got older I compensated by having other people find things for me. How often had I looked for something on my desk only to have my nurse, Donna, come in and find it right in front of me?

Hearing

Sometimes Joshua only heard parts of things. Often he would say, "What?" and I would repeat what I had said, assuming that he hadn't heard me. In my new questioning mode I would say, "Tell me what you think you heard." I was shocked to find that most of the time Joshua had heard exactly what I said. Why he said "What?" he did not know, and neither did I. One thing was clear to me, though. He operated on two levels. He could listen on one and say "what" on the other. Then there were other times when he heard nothing on either level. Yet he could be playing a game in his room with the radio blasting and he would hear a whisper in the hallway.

It wasn't clear if he did not hear something or if he was just listening on one level while operating on another. I noticed that it seemed easier for him to operate on two or three levels than one.

Smell And Taste

I did not have to ask Joshua about smell because it was abundantly obvious. He had a super-acute sense of smell and could not stand the smell of most foods. That was part of the reason that he only ate bread and water. But I knew that was only part of the story. For some reason he was hypersensitive to taste, apart from smell. Sometimes he held his nose in the hope that he would be able to eat certain things, but he would just vomit.

Touch

Joshua had very strange reactions to the sense of touch, which included pain, heat, cold, contact, and pressure.

Pain was the most obvious. He did not seem to experience pain in the same way as other children. When he fell on the playground he did not cry, even if he scraped himself badly. When he got his shots or had his blood drawn he was fascinated but he never cried. It was as if he did not feel it.

His reactions to hot and cold were also unusual. In middle of the winter Joshua could walk out with almost nothing on and never complain about the cold. I rarely felt the need for a coat in the winter so it didn't seem like a big deal to me. On really cold days Ellen or I would ask him to put on a coat and he would happily do so. At one time he so liked the feel of one winter coat, that he began wearing it daily. He even wanted to wear it in the summer. We had to be firm that he could not wear a winter coat during the summer. When the winter rolled around again he would sometimes wear his coat, but not because of the cold—he just liked the way it felt.

Joshua's response to pressure was perhaps the oddest because while he seemed to feel no pain, he could be driven crazy by something exerting pressure on his skin. The tag in the back of his shirt could drive him wild, so we had to remove them. If his sock was not perfectly placed in his shoe, he would have to fix it until it felt right. On the other hand, he was perfectly happy to walk around without shoes. It did not matter what time of year or what kind of surface. He could walk on hot tar or gravel.

There was one particular event that surprised me. His class went on a school trip and we gave him a dollar as the teacher had requested. When he came home we asked him if he spent it. He managed to explain that he bought candy and that he got change. When we asked where it was, he took off his shoe and showed us. He had been walking on five or six coins all day and it did not seem to bother him. But if his sock was not placed exactly the way he liked it in his shoes he would be inconsolable.

One thing became obvious about Joshua's senses. His sensory input was different from most people's. He felt things that others did not, and he did not feel things that others did. He sometimes seemed to be sensorially lacking, but sometimes his senses were hyperacute.

One winter morning he put on his socks, underpants, and shirt and waited for me outside the door wearing a winter coat and his backpack. He had no shoes and no pants. I stared at him incredulously and said,

"Are you ready to go to school?"

"Yes."

"Are you forgetting anything?"

"No."

"Are you sure?"

"Yes."

"Where are your shoes and pants?"

He looked down and he said, "Whoopsy."

I asked, "Didn't you realize you had no shoes or pants?"

"I thought I did," he responded.

As I waited for Joshua to put on his pants and shoes I shook my head and thought about how he missed the obvious but made connections that went beyond what children are usually able to understand, like when my friend Larry's wife, Vanessa, died.

When Vanessa developed cancer, I was the doctor who told Larry. I also told Joshua. Vanessa seemed to like and understand Joshua. She was only forty-two when she died. Joshua was three. She was the first person Joshua had ever known who had died, and he had an insatiable curiosity about it. He was deeply affected, and struggled mightily to understand her death. We talked about it night after night in place of his bedtime story. His struggle to understand the importance and ramifications of death were, I thought, extraordinary. He asked about, and seemed to understand, the terrible sadness that Larry felt. He thought about what it meant for Vanessa's parents, and how it impacted him and me. He struggled to understand how death fit into the world.

It was not only his depth of feeling that amazed me, but also his insight. He asked me if I missed *my* daddy, who had also died young. He wished aloud that he had met my father, so that he would have had some memories of him to treasure. He was sorry for my father, who never enjoyed even a few moments of happiness with his grandson before he died. He hoped aloud that I would not die precipitously, like my father, and that his mother, Ellen, would not die like Vanessa. He seemed to understand the sadness of losing a father or a wife. I knew that this was unusual for such a young child and I was very proud of him. How, I wondered, could this be the same child who forgot to put on his pants and shoes.

I searched for a diagnosis that would fit Joshua and I found that many of his sensory issues were shared with children with who had Sensory Integration Dysfunction or ADD or were learning disabled, but I was on a mission to teach him to read and I did not find help with those diagnoses— I needed to take action.

Each evening we would adjourn to his room to talk, read stories and tickle each other while I searched for clues on how to teach him. We worked on his communication skills by my getting him to talk about things in a fun, nonpressure situation. I noticed that Joshua sensed that he made others uncomfortable when he spoke. His stammering embarrassed him, as did forgetting what he was saying midsentence. When he managed to tell a whole story, his strange sequencing made it difficult to understand the links from sentence to sentence. He had become used to people interrupting and finishing his sentences for him; however, I never did that at our nightly meetings. I waited patiently for him to finish. He disliked having to complete his sentences and thoughts, but he did it. I interspersed tickling and reading stories with my incessant questioning and mostly we had fun. The only thing I really didn't enjoy was reading to him.

Joshua did not know that I really disliked reading bedtime stories. Reading children's books made me even more fidgety than Joshua—and he was very fidgety. I could hardly pay attention to my reading because I was always thinking about something else and losing my place. One night after I finished a pullout book about Spot the dog, I perfunctorily asked Joshua if he understood what I had just read. What followed was my first real breakthrough.

"Did you understand the story?"

Shaking his head from side to side and avoiding my gaze, he said, "No," rather sheepishly.

"Where did you get lost?" I asked casually.

"In the top."

I knew what he meant by the top. He meant the beginning.

"Do you remember which page?"

He shook his head no and looked away. I knew I was on to something here. Joshua was clearly embarrassed about that question and I did not understand why. I leafed backward, page-by-page, and asked him if he remembered each page. I got blank stares until we got to the title page. It was difficult to not be emotionally overwhelmed. I hated reading books and I was doing this for him. I was reading all the parts in different voices and trying to be animated and make it fun. And Joshua had not heard any of it.

Understanding some of the exasperation of his teachers and trying to conceal my frustration, I reread the book, trying to do as good a job the second time. I then asked him the same question: "Did you follow it this time?"

Again he shook his head, no.

"Where did you get lost?"

He just shrugged.

Once again I laboriously leafed backward through the book. I was relieved to see that this time he registered familiarity on page four. I read the remaining pages again. When we got to the end this time, Joshua took the initiative. He thumbed back two pages and pointed and looked at me. I understood and I read the last two pages again. Suddenly, it hit me—Joshua was just like me. He needed repetition because his mind would wander. I stopped and asked him what he was thinking about. He said monsters, and battles, his dreams of being famous or really smart, or being a doctor like me. Frankly, I found his imaginings more interesting than the story we were reading. It made sense to me that this was one reason that Joshua was blocking certain sensory input, but it did not explain everything. There were things that were blocked from his field of vision and things he did not hear or feel. But there were contradictions that I could not understand. How could a slightly twisted sock bother him, yet walking on a shoe full of coins not? I was perplexed. I knew I had a lot of work to do.

chapter eight

Learning Begins

As I pored over books designed for early readers and texts for teaching children the alphabet, I began to realize that the educational and publishing establishments had, for many years, canonized what was "easy" to learn and what was "hard." However, Joshua had a different experience of "easy" and "hard."

"What is this letter?" I would say, pointing to an *a*. "What is that letter?" I would ask, pointing to another letter. It was painfully slow, but at least Joshua could recognize about twelve letters, and he knew their sounds. But there were many letters that, no matter how much repetition we did, he could not seem to get. Sometimes he would seem to learn them and then the next day it would be like starting over.

One night while reading a book, I pointed to the word

finger and asked him to say the letters in the word. I knew that he was really good at *f* so I thought picking a word that began with a letter he knew well would give him confidence. When I pointed to the *f* he said, *"fuh."*

"Terrific," I said, and I saw that he was very proud of himself.

"What is the next letter?" I asked, knowing that he always had trouble with the letter *i*. He was always getting confused: *ih* or *eye*. I was shocked when, without hesitation, he said, *"Ing."*

"Why did you say *ing*?" I asked. He shrugged his shoulders in response.

"How do you know that says *ing*?" I asked again.

Again I got the shoulder shrug. I searched the page for another word with *ing* in it, and I pointed to it and asked, "What is this?"

"Ing," he said.

"Okay," I said, "show me all of the places that you see *ing*."

Stunned and delighted, I watched as he turned page after page pointing out *ing*. I remember being amazed at how many *ings* there were.

"Can you show me all the *I*'s?" I asked him.

Silence.

Hmm, I thought and I bolted out of his room and quickly retrieved a newspaper. I said. "Draw a line under *ing* everywhere you see it."

The difference between a circle and a line had always

eluded Joshua and this time was no exception. He began circling words that had *ing*.

"Keep doing it," I said.

I ran to my computer and typed all the words with *ing* in them that started with letters I knew that Joshua knew, and printed it out. It looked exactly like this, except on a full 8.5" × 11" page.

Bing

Jing

King

Ming

Ping

Ring

Zing

Bing, jing, king, ming. Joshua could read *ing* and I was thrilled with this revelation. It was getting late and Ellen said he should really be going to sleep. "Okay," I said and kissed him good night, trying to contain my excitement as I left his room.

I was too excited to sit down. I knew I had discovered something really important, although I wasn't quite sure what it was. I went out for a walk to try to calm down, but it barely helped. When I returned I sat down at my computer and attempted to organize my thoughts, and to understand what had just happened.

I needed to figure out how to capitalize on the breakthrough. I thought if he could read *ing*, then maybe he could read *ang* or *ong* or *eng* and so on. I immediately set to making lists of words that had these sounds in them. I wrote *ing* on the top of the page and wrote all the words down that I could think of that had *ing* in them, and then did the same for *ong*. Suddenly I realized that I needed a good dictionary.

"Be right back," I said to Ellen, "Gotta go to the bookstore."

"Now?" she asked. "It's 10:30 at night."

"I know," I said, "but Barnes & Noble is open until midnight every night." I flew out the door and virtually skipped to Barnes & Noble. Unable to wait for the elevator, I shot up the steps two and three at a time.

As I arrived at the dictionary section I was amazed at the variety available. Despite being in an ecstasy-fueled mania, I drew the line at buying the gargantuan *Oxford Unabridged Dictionary*—I did not want a hernia. I spent the next hour and a half scrutinizing the rest of the dictionaries. When I heard the announcement over the loudspeaker that the store would close in ten minutes, I chose five or six of my favorites, paid for them, and almost ran home. Ellen was asleep as I tiptoed into the living room and booted up my computer.

I set up a new folder and named it READ. I created five different documents, which I called *ing, ong, ung, eng,* and *ang*. I opened one document at a time and wrote the name of the file at the top of the page. *Ing* was my first. I opened the dictionaries, looking for words that had *ing* in them. I realized that most dictionaries did not classify words by phonemes or blends like *ing*. With the rhyming dictionary I hit pay dirt. In fact, it was too good. There were too many words that had *ing* in them. How would I decide which *ing* words to put on my page? Then I decided to do what I should have done in the first place. I got some children's books and typed each word I found in a book that had the word *ing* in it. I figured that I could then read the book with him, and he could read *ing*.

When I got to *ung* I suddenly remembered something. When working with Joshua on the vowels using repetition, kindness, and fun, we spent nearly two weeks on the letter *U* and he still wasn't all that good at recognizing or sounding it. How was he going to learn *ung*, which started with a *u*? Then I remembered that he had trouble with the letter *i*, and he read *ing*.

It was now 5:30 in the morning. I crawled into bed only to be awakened ninety minutes later by the stirring of the house. Ellen got up and came back to the bedroom with a puzzled look on her face.

"What were you doing last night? There are papers and new dictionaries everywhere."

"Oh just some stuff to work on for Joshua. Don't worry, I'll clean it up."

I was too tired to get up, and I fell back to sleep for another two hours. Ellen woke me up to ask me if I was sick. It was not like me to be so tired in the morning. I told her I was fine. She had already taken Joshua to school. As I dressed and left hurriedly for the office, I was upset with myself for falling back to sleep. I was eager to try out my lists on Joshua.

When I got to my office I cancelled all non-emergency patients and rescheduled the others close together because I wanted to meet Joshua after school. I got to his school a half hour early and realized that I had forgotten my lists. No matter, as soon as Joshua emerged I took his hand and whisked him away. We got home and I immediately got my lists. I chose *ing* first. I did it in green because I knew it was Joshua's favorite color. First I said show where it says *ing*. He pointed each one out. How did you know that, I asked? "The puter," he said. So I took him over to the "puter" so he could show me. He pointed to one of his favorite games, "Treasure Mountain." In the game there is a question for teaching the sound *ing* by pointing to it and then saying it out loud.

"You can read," I shouted. "Joshua, you can read!"

Joshua had absolutely no idea what I was talking about.

"No," he said.

"Yes, you can. That *is* reading. Let me show you."

We went into his room and closed the door and I got out my lists.

Although Joshua could not read any of my other lists such as *ung, ang, eng, ong*, he could read *ing* and the words on my sheet that began with the letters that he knew.

"Okay," I said, "let's try and learn another little word."

We were on a roll. The juices were flowing and there was

enough human electricity in that room to melt the ice on the North Pole. We were laughing, tickling, and virtually bouncing off the walls. We were having a great time.

"You see," I said, "reading is fun." He nodded vigorously as he jumped up and down on his bed over and over.

Next we tried *ang*. I asked, "What is this?"

"*ang*," Joshua said.

I asked him again.

No answer.

"*ang*," I said.

"What is this?"

"*ang*," he said.

"What is this?"

"*ang*," he repeated.

"What is this?"

"*ang*," he said.

"What is this?" I said, pointing to *ing*.

"*ing*," he said.

After two hours we were both a little batty, but Joshua was pretty good at remembering *ang*. When I tried to get him to distinguish between *ing* and *ang* he could get it right most of the time. We were both excited.

I told Ellen what had happened and while she thought it was great she did not understand why we had to get so wild. Neither did I, but we did.

I was really tired so I sat down on the couch only to wake up a few hours later at 8:30 P.M. Ellen asked me again if I was okay. I told her I felt great. The kids were asleep so I went directly to my computer. I realized that I needed index cards, and I remembered that Staples was open till 9:00, so I told Ellen I would be right back.

"Where are you going?"

"To get index cards."

"Now?"

When I got to Staples I was thrilled to see they stocked a staggering assortment of index cards. I bought 3" × 5", and 5" × 7". I bought them in every color they had: green, red, blue, yellow, purple, and white, lined and unlined. They also had neon colors and I bought a couple of multicolored packs of those. I rushed home and began typing up index cards with *ing, ang,* and so on. Then I typed up cards with the words from my sheets that had those sounds in them such as *bing, bang, bung, king kong, ding dong.*

I printed words on every color card in big print, small print, and five different fonts, and in blue, red, and green ink. I had a stack of index cards like the ones I had made to study for medical board exams. It was 4:30 in the morning. I crawled into bed only to awaken at 8:30 and find that Joshua had already left for school. I called my office and told my nurse to make only emergency appointments for that day and the rest of the week. I told her I was not feeling quite right, which was true, though in some way I was feeling more right than I had in a very long time.

I got up, went to the office, and worked past nine that night. When I came home the kids were asleep and Ellen was watching television. I said "Hi," and sat down at the computer. Ellen said, "Are you going to work all night again?" "No" I said. And then I did. But the next morning I was ready. I had been through sleeplessness before as an intern. Of course I was almost twenty years older now, but I knew what it took, and I knew I could do it. I had set the alarm on my watch and was armed and ready with my index cards when I took Joshua to school. As soon as we got outside I showed him the first card. "*ing*," he said. The next he said "*ang*" and I alternated between two cards, *ing* and *ang*. We took a few moments' break in between the cards for tickling, but by the time we got to school, he seemed to have mastered those two cards. As I watched Joshua bound up the school steps I figured that this was about as good as life gets on this planet. Joshua and I were on to something and there would be no stopping us now. I knew it and Joshua knew it.

Over the next few days Joshua learned to read *ang, eng, ing, ong,* and *ung* but strangely he still could not identify the letters *a, e, i, o, u* with any consistency. For some reason *ang* was easier for him to read than the letter *a*.

I made up more cards with *ast, est, ist, ost,* and *ust*. Again he seemed to be able to read those although he was still having trouble with *a, e, i, o, u*.

Because Joshua had trouble with the traditional alphabet, I thought I would make him one of his own. I started a new file and wrote on top of the page ALPHABET TOO.

I started with *ing*. It was not a letter, but it was clearly recognized by Joshua as such. I added all the other letters and blends and letter groups that I felt he recognized as letters. I added the regular alphabet letters that he could master, such as *b, p, r,* and made up a few others like *qu* (qwuh) but no *q.* I also added *ph.* I found it strange that the letters in the word *cat* totally befuddled Joshua. It did not make sense to me that he could recognize certain letter combinations such as *ing* but had trouble with a single letter like *c.* I knew that difference in understanding was a key to helping him learn to read.

Every day our "Alphabet Too" was growing. There were index cards strewn everywhere—Joshua's bedroom, my bedroom, the living room, and the kitchen. Ellen definitely did not like the mess but she was happy to see us happy and to see Joshua learning. She was even getting in on the fun by going over cards with Joshua. Aaron was jealous, so we made up some cards for him and he was having fun, too.

I was now in the habit of sleeping from 6–8 P.M. and then staying up all night making new and more elaborate cards for our ever-expanding alphabet. I added *at, et ot, it* and *ut,* and *an, in, on, un,* and *en* and then went for the double *ll* combinations *all, ell, ill, ull, oll.* Joshua could now read lots of words. *King Kong, ding dong, best, pest, nest, bell, tall, call,* and more. But there were some letters that he found impossibly difficult and could not learn. Those letters were *a, e, i, o,* and *u* as well as *t, d, c* and some others. I made a list of the letters Joshua could not learn and desperately sought to discover some commonality among them.

Easy and Hard

It occurred to me that the problems Joshua had with many letters (and therefore with words) was that many letters have different sounds under different circumstances. I think that Joshua was able to get a handle on *ing*, *ang*, and so on because they sounded the same under all circumstances. A letter like *c*, however, could be pronounced numerous ways even though it always looked the same. For example, *cat* is usually regarded as a simple word, but Joshua struggled with it. On the other hand, *bring*, which had his familiar friend *ing* in it, was easy for Joshua. I decided to compare *cat* and *bring* and discovered how a simple word isn't so simple.

1. CAT
2. BRING

CAT

1. C
2. A
3. T

C

C can be pronounced in many different ways. It can be hard and sound just like a *k*. When you look at the word you immediately start out saying "cuh," which is the first sound in *cat*. Or do you say "s," like in *cereal*?

A

A is pretty simple. Everyone knows the *a* sound. It is "ah" like in apple. Or is it "a" as in ape. Or perhaps it is *"aw"* like in all?

T

T can also have a number of pronunciations. It can also be confused with words that end in *ed* (*worked* sounds like it ends in *t*). *The* doesn't even sound like it has a *t* in it at all.

So is the word *cat* easy? No! *Cat* is a hard word.

Let's look at *bring*. It's not a common word in early readers because it is a complex word. Right? Wrong!

BRING

1. B
2. R
3. ING

B

I can only think of one way to say a *b*. It's "buh." There are no other possibilities except "buh."

R

R sounds the same in any word I can think of. In *word, clearing, run, right, further, Bruce.*

ING

The third and last letter in the word bring is *ing*

Yes, *ing* is a letter in the "Alphabet Too." Not only is it a letter, it is a letter that can only be said only one way, which means it is the easiest kind of letter to learn.

It might take a learning disabled child a week to learn one difficult letter. The easy letters could be learned faster. The educational system insists that letters like *c* and *t* are easy, and when kids struggle with them the system labels these children as having a learning problem. In fact, it is not a learning problem, but a teaching problem. In fact, it is easier to teach some children the letters *ing* or *all* or *th* than to teach them the letter *c*. Joshua and kids like him need to learn these letters before they start to read or it will make the learning process unbearable.

When words are classified by some of the different sounds of all the letters (variables), it allows for a new and easier way to classify what is easy and what is hard. *Cat* is hard and *bring* is easy. The following chart helps to illustrate the differences.

Joshua could still only read what I considered easy letters, and I needed to teach him the hard letters, such as the vowels. Pondering the differences between the easy letters and the hard letters, their common denominator was obvious:

	BRING	CAT
number of letters	5	3
level of difficulty of letters	easy	hard

explanation of level of difficulty	B one way letter
	R one way letter
	ING one way letter
		C intersection letter
		➤ can be said in two totally different ways
		  1. "suh"
		  2. "cuh"
		➤ sounds like other letters—*k*
		➤ changes pronunciation when combined with *h*, The *ch* combination creates a different sound than regular *c*.
		
		A intersection letter
		➤ can be said in two primary ways
		  1. long "ay"
		  2. short "ah"
		➤ and a variety of lesser ways.
		  "Aw," and in *all*
		
		T intersection letter
		➤ Pronounced differently depending on situations
		  1. "th"
		  2. "itch"
		  3. "tuh"
		➤ easily confused with other letters *d* and *ed* for example, *passed/past*

Easy letters could only be pronounced one way. Hard letters could be pronounced more than one way. The more ways a letter could be pronounced, the harder the letter. There had to be a way to break down the hard letters so that they became a series of easy letters. I needed a model that I could use to help Joshua learn. The model would incorporate what I had learned so far from working with Joshua:

1. Joshua loved cars, so I would try to involve cars.

2. It had to accommodate all of the letters of the new alphabet that Joshua and I had been compiling.

3. It had to allow for incremental increases in difficulty without changing the paradigm.

There simply did not seem to be enough hours in the day, so I decided I would sleep from 8–10 P.M., wake up and work until about 5 A.M., and then try to get an hour of sleep before going to work. Ellen was unhappy about the hours I was keeping but she saw that Joshua could read numerous words and she was eager to see more progress. Explanations of my theories about hard and easy, letters and words made her nervous but she was encouraged because Joshua and I were making headway.

Weeks passed and although Ellen was concerned about my not sleeping, she continued to be more upset about my not paying enough attention to Aaron because I was so focused on teaching Joshua to read. She was right. I was already overwhelmed with guilt about it, and her expression of concern exacerbated those feelings.

Aaron was in many ways like Ellen. He was calm, cool, and collected, and demanded very little. He was now two and hardly ever cried or made a sound. He was changing from week to week, characteristic of that age. I knew that I was being obsessive about teaching Joshua to read, and I knew it was really important, but I also realized that I did not want to miss Aaron growing up. I decided that I would devote every Tuesday exclusively to Aaron. We would do stuff just like Joshua and I used to do. Aaron, however, was much lower maintenance than Joshua. All I needed to do to make Aaron happy was hug and kiss him. That became our favorite Tuesday activity. Aaron would often ask if it was Tuesday. He couldn't wait for his day to hug and kiss. On Tuesday morning when I got up, all I would have to say was "Time to hug and kiss on the couch," and he would run to the couch and jump up, just waiting to hug and kiss. It was great. I would also cook for him on Tuesdays, and unlike Ellen and Joshua, he enjoyed new and interesting foods. I was thrilled that he appreciated my cooking. He also liked going shopping with me and walking slowly, looking at things. We were developing our own special activities and interests to communicate about, and a close bond was forming. Then something happened that really shocked Ellen and me and about which we were conflicted.

We went to visit my mother. Ellen and I were very proud of how well Joshua was doing, and so was Joshua. My mother had a small statue of a horse in her room that she had given Aaron to play with. Aaron came in to sit down with us, and my mother asked him to get the horse from her room and show Mommy and Daddy. Unlike Joshua, who moved like the wind, Aaron stood up slowly, lumbered out of the room, and returned with a book in his hand. We had been through this kind of stuff before with Joshua. But confusing a book and a horse still was a quite a stretch—until I saw the title of the book. It was *A Man Called Horse*, and there was not picture of a horse anywhere to be found on the cover or anywhere else. We sat in silence and looked at each other. Aaron had just done something extraordinary for a two-and-a-half-year-old child, yet we were all thinking about how this would affect Joshua.

I considered not teaching Aaron things as a way to protect Joshua from a brother who was almost four years younger and might soon overtake him scholastically. The very thought of that scared me. But it was clear that Aaron was going to be a front rower just like his mother, and he was capable of learning on his own. I was tormented by the fact that I actually considered denying Aaron the same effort at teaching him things as Joshua. But Aaron seemed fine. He was clearly not suffering. Finally I spoke to Ellen about it. She agreed it was a difficult situation, but she was certainly not tormented. She was never tormented. She said, "You will just have to teach Joshua to read faster." I was shocked. I was beginning to break through to her. Then she added, "But can you do it without staying up all night?"

"I don't think so," I answered.

I went back to work on figuring out how to teach Joshua the letters that he did not know, like the vowels. I was having trouble coming up with a good paradigm, so I thought that I should try and analyze my own life to see what clues I could uncover that might be useful in teaching Joshua.

chapter nine

The Past Is the Key to the Present

As I searched my memories of my learning triumphs and failures it occurred to me that I had misunderstood the significance of some of the most critical times of my life. During those times I proved to myself that I could learn as well as, or even better than, others. Now I examined those times through the critical eyes of a trained physician, hoping to better understand the nature of Joshua's problems in order to treat them. There were two learning experiences that I remembered most vividly, and I was certain they contained useful clues.

Abnormal Psychology

After flirting with music and English in college, I finally found something that I really enjoyed: psychology. Abnormal psychology was considered the weeding-out course for anyone who wanted to major in psychology, just as organic chemistry did for medical school, so I signed up for it.

Like many classes at the State University of New York at Stony Brook, there were hundreds of students in the class and so it was held in a large lecture hall, where the teacher stood at the front of the class. Although this allowed for an uninterrupted field of vision, it meant that the students in the last row could not hear the teacher without a microphone, and it was unlikely the teacher could actually discern faces or see a raised hand. To compensate, the teacher's notes were projected onto three large movie-size screens so that they could be seen easily. While the layout was certainly not conducive to individual attention from the teacher, it was educational nirvana for me. The teacher would not know if I was doodling or if my mind wandered.

There were rumors that the teacher was a brilliant young star on the fast track. He was publishing a lot and had some interesting new ideas about teaching. He seemed straightforward: Attend the lectures, read the book, and learn the material, and you would ace the exam.

I usually enjoyed going to class, and I found the textbook fascinating and unusually well written. I utilized the strategies that I had developed over the years for reading a textbook. I used colored highlighters, notes to myself written in the margins, and circled and underlined things when I re-read them. I even tore some pages out and taped them to my wall to help in memorization. Occasionally I had to re-read one hundred pages or more over because I missed the point the first time around. While this was not time efficient and made for a well worn book, I came to know the material very well.

As the course entered its third week it was impossible not to notice that class attendance had diminished considerably. I assumed that was because the book was so good and his lectures were so bad. The teacher noticed the same thing. Then he dropped a bomb: A significant percentage of the exams would be based on the material in his lectures. Suddenly the room was filled for every class, and everyone sat furiously scribbling class notes. I had no class notes.

I could not take notes. I had never been able to. It required an uninterrupted focus and the ability to transfer ideas from my head to paper in a way I simply could not master. I would daydream a little, doodle, doze off, or pass notes to my girlfriend. I did, however, keep up with my book reading. As the day of the test approached, I became anxious. In spite of how hard I had studied, I was afraid that I would do poorly on my exam because I did not possess the little test tidbits he had casually tossed out during lectures, during which I was often daydreaming.

Suddenly the test was upon me and I felt the need to take some type of action.

I asked a girl who I knew was a compulsive note taker and had excellent penmanship if I could borrow her class notes to study for the test. She was very straight-laced and normally would have said no to such a request, but she knew me and she knew how well I knew the material. She said I could have her notes after she went to sleep at 11 P.M. on the night before the exam. That presented a problem—I was not good at staying awake at night, and I figured that it would take me at least five or six hours to just read the notes one time.

Many of my classmates drank coffee and took caffeine pills sold over the counter to pull all-nighters. They also took diet pills. I hated coffee, so I decided to take a diet pill. The one I took was an amphetamine chemically related to Ritalin, which I had learned about in Abnormal Psych. It was used to treat hyperactive children. I knew that I was a little hyperactive; I was a bit worried that the pill would make me *really* hyperactive, but I tried it anyway.

Eleven P.M. arrived. I took the diet pill, picked up the class notes, and settled in for a long night of studying. A very odd thing happened, however. The pill made me so tired that I quickly realized I would never be able to stay up all night. I decided to simply go through the notes as fast as I could and go to sleep accepting that I would probably do poorly on the test.

As I started to study, though, I was startled to note that I was making astonishing headway. I was moving at an uncanny rate of speed. Moreover, I felt no need to reread and

I seemed to be retaining the information. I assumed that these were either the best notes on the face of the earth or I was in some sort of semi-delusional drugged state. Nevertheless, I kept going and after about two and a half hours I simply closed the notebook, returned it, and went to sleep.

My alarm clock went off and I felt terrible. Although I had slept I did not feel rested and could hardly keep my eyes open. I was worried that I would not be able to remember what I had read in the abnormal psychology textbook. I went to class angry with myself for taking the drug and upset that I was unable to take notes of my own.

As I walked into the test and sat down, I rested my head on my arms, desperately trying not to fall asleep. How, I thought, could people take these drugs to stay awake? I was too tired to even think about it. As I watched the teacher at the front of the class, handing the test papers to the first person in each row, and then each student methodically passing the papers to the students behind them, I was struck with a familiar feeling: hoping I was not going to be left back—again. I was relieved to see that it was a multiple-choice exam. At least I would have a fighting chance, providing I could finish it (something I rarely did with a multiple-choice test.)

I looked at the first question. It was an easy one—straight out of the notes. I had the same feeling about the second question, and the third. After the first ten questions I realized that I recalled the answers to all of them. They were the esoteric tidbits I had originally been so worried about.

I was the first person to finish the test, which made me very nervous. I scanned the room and saw two hundred students still struggling. This had never happened to me before. I was *always* the last one to finish. Could it have been because my friend had taken such great notes? I would have to thank her profusely. As I walked to the front of the room, test paper in hand, I passed her and noticed that she was in the middle of the test. Now I was *really* nervous and began to have a familiar feeling of impending doom. I knew she was a smart and a conscientious student. But I was too tired to worry about it and I handed in my paper. The teacher was impressed.

"So did you do well?" he asked.

"I think so, but maybe I just don't know how little I know," I said.

I rushed back to my room and went directly to sleep.

I was surprised at the next class when the teacher held up one paper and asked, "So, who is Bruce Roseman?" As I stood up and our eyes met, he nodded at me, clearly remembering that I had finished my exam earlier than everybody else. "You got the highest grade in the class."

At the end of my abnormal psychology course, the teacher approached me and told me about a new teaching method he was working on for the next semester. It would be a different and exciting way to teach, and would be particularly suited to a school like Stony Brook with large classes. He asked me if I was interested in assisting him with teaching, organizing, and writing some of the exams. I was honored to be offered such an opportunity and was determined to do a good job. I told him that I would work on it all summer and repay his faith in me.

The method was quite simple. A number of different teachers would give lectures but the tests would come directly from the textbook. There would be thirty separate tests. If you passed all of the tests you got an A, twenty-five passes for a B, twenty passes for a C, fifteen passes for a D, and with anything less than fifteen you failed. It was rather straightforward, except that these tests were not scored quantitatively. They were graded pass or fail, and if you failed you could take the test again and again and until you passed. Someone who had already taken the course and mastered the material administered the tests. It was the job of the tester to not simply administer and grade the test, but also to teach the student the information that they got wrong on the test. The point was that someone was trying to ascertain the specific weakness of each student and then teaching to correct that weakness.

Some people passed all of the tests with ease; some had to take each test three or four times. The people who passed the tests easily learned more of the curriculum quickly, but the slower students could still do well through diligence. The lazy students were the ones who really suffered. They would just stop whenever they got the grade they found acceptable. The important point though, was that even the students who learned less actually *knew what they had learned*. This was in sharp contrast to the way that teaching was generally done, and the way that Joshua was currently being taught—a test was given, and if you passed you moved on regardless of how much you did *not* know. If you failed, you were not given the time or the teaching to learn the material you did not know.

That summer, I began studying my abnormal psychology book and dissecting it page by page. I wrote up tests for each chapter. I also prepared a few lectures on the off chance that he would allow me to give them. I discovered something very important from that experience: Even though I thought that I knew my abnormal psychology pretty well the more I thought about teaching it to others, the better I understood it. Moreover, in order to teach it to others, I had to anticipate what they would find difficult. The goal was to not catch them to make them fail, but rather to catch them to make sure they understood. My experience with this class helped me to understand how I had to teach Joshua to read. I needed to use constant repetition and multidimensional representation of the information, and I had to teach him in a way that I thought would prepare him to teach it to others. I had to teach him to anticipate every possible problem that other people would have in order to improve his own understanding.

Physics

Physics had been the bane of my existence in high school. After a few classes it was immediately apparent to me and to my teacher that I would *never* pass. I dropped it twice in high school and avoided it in college—until that fateful day that I decided to become a doctor.

In my senior year of college, about to graduate with a degree in psychology, with minors in English and music, I suddenly decided that I wanted to be a doctor. I had met with extraordinary success after my first year of school and believed for the first time in my life that I was a good student. I reasoned that if I could master my other courses, there must be some way I could pass physics, which was essential for medical school. I assumed it would be difficult and boring, but I was more determined than ever.

It had been two years since my success with abnormal psychology and a year since I had helped teach the class. I heard that one teacher was now teaching physics in the same way that I had taught abnormal psychology. I went to speak to the teacher, who was also the author of the textbook used in the class. I dropped by the physics lab and found him alone and at work. I had a lot of preconceived notions about physics and teachers, but this man seemed different. He listened carefully to my tale of physics woes. He then took the time to patiently explain to me why he had organized this physics course in this way. I came away feeling that if I was ever going to pass a physics course this would be the one. I also understood that this was my last chance: Pass this class or forget about medical school.

I signed up for the course and was assigned to a teaching assistant who would perform the same function that I had performed for abnormal psychology. It was his job to administer each of the twenty-five tests and to make sure that I understood and passed each test before I could move on to the next one.

My teaching assistant was an Australian doctoral student who was well known in the physics community as an incredibly demanding teacher who would often pontificate about how American students did not appreciate the tremendous opportunities they were offered. He also tended to give out poor grades. Everybody tried to avoid him like the plague. I was late to sign up for a teaching assistant and had no idea of what constituted a good or bad physics teacher, so I was assigned to him. I went to meet him and thought he seemed like a nice enough fellow who clearly loved physics. I mentioned to him that I had spoken to Dr. S about the way the course was taught and mentioned my experience with this teaching method. He made it clear that he did not agree with the method because he thought it was too easy and prevented true competition, which he considered a good thing. Less competition sounded good to me, as did phrases like "too easy." I arranged to take my first test with him in two days.

From the outset, physics was very difficult. I had studied for about a week and struggled though it, and was hoping I knew enough to get by. I was totally wrong. In fact, when I took the test the teaching assistant told me that I had absolutely no understanding of what I had just studied. He recommended that I drop the course because he thought it unlikely that I could ever pass. I told the teacher I would think about it and let him know the next day.

I decided that if I really studied hard I could get it and returned the following week to retake the test. The teacher was surprised to see me but was impressed that I had returned. Unfortunately, I failed the test again. This time I decided to make the most of the advantage of this type of course. I asked him if he would explain my mistakes. He had no other students and seemed happy to spend two hours explaining the material to me. I went home to study what he had taught me. I had a far better understanding of the material, but I was still confused by some things. I went back the next day and he explained some more, and he continued to do so each day I returned. I was now spending hours every day with him in what amounted to one-on-one tutoring.

After three weeks I finally passed the first of twenty-five tests. I was very proud of myself and it was clear that he was too. He told me that I understood the physics for that first test better than any student he had ever given the test to. That was the good news. The bad news was that even though he was very impressed with how I had mastered the material, it was only the first chapter of the book. I would need to pass fourteen more tests in order to get a D, and there was simply not enough time in the semester for that. Once again, he suggested that I drop the course.

I decided that since things were going so well I would just keep doing what I was doing. He told me that in order to survive the course, I needed to learn more math. It was obvious that I was very poor at multiplication and division, and I needed to learn trigonometry.

Learning to multiply and divide was relatively simple. Although I had never learned the multiplication and division tables before, I committed them to memory now. Trigonometry was another story; I had flunked in both high school and college. I decided to start at the beginning and bought a high school review text on trigonometry and set to reading it that very night. It was a revelation. I found that doing it in my own way and in my own time and repeating a sentence or page or chapter as many as five or six times made all the difference in the world to my understanding the material. Over the next thirty-six hours I read and studied that trigonometry book, taking time to nap and eat only when absolutely necessary. As I approached the end of the book I realized something that astonished me. I had mastered in hours what I could not learn in a full year of high school and in a full semester of college trigonometry. How could that be? I realized that the key to my success was that I could move at my own speed and in my own way without being judged every step of the way.

Armed with my newly acquired math smarts, the physics was much easier to comprehend. It took me only one week to pass my next test, and in the following week I passed three tests. The teacher had never seen anyone pass three tests in one week; he was amazed even though I had taken about twenty hours per week of private tutoring. Since few students felt the need for individual help, he was happy to work with me to pass the time. I was grateful for the attention, the value of which was priceless.

By the time I got to the twentieth test, the dynamics of our relationship had changed dramatically. He told me that I was the best physics student he had ever seen, and that I should go on and complete a physics major and then go to graduate school for a Ph.D. in physics. He offered to help me get in, which I appreciated and even briefly considered. I had developed a real love of physics but being a doctor seemed like it would be more fun.

The Australian doctoral student's patience in explaining the material from all different angles so that I could understand it, never moving on until I understood everything in its totality, made me realize that I was never bad at physics. I simply needed to learn it differently from most people. I did not have a learning problem; all the teachers who had come before him had a teaching problem.

The patience of that physics teacher, coupled with an unusual teaching method, were the essential reasons for my success. I realized I could apply these techniques to working with Joshua: Joshua could be me, reading could be physics, and I could be that physics teacher. This approach was labor intensive because it required explaining the material in many different ways until the best way was discovered, and then explaining it over and over again.

As I considered the various ways to present information, I remembered the double helix of Watson and Crick, which revealed the secrets of DNA. This great discovery was contingent on conceptualizing the double helix in three dimensions. I knew that teaching Joshua was not a three dimensional situation, so I decided to look for other ways to add dimensions to teaching. I could use color, size, order, catchy phrases, and whatever else I could think of. I started experimenting with a variety of visual presentations. I reviewed my lists of letters, what was easy and hard, and what Joshua knew and didn't know. I spent every moment looking for patterns, experimenting with paradigms, and establishing hypotheses, theorems, and ever new and more unusual ways to teach Joshua letters in our unusual alphabet.

I was able to focus on my current patients although I was no longer interested in taking on new ones. I withdrew from the everyday world in every other aspect, but I believed that I was getting close to putting everything together for Joshua. I thought things were going swimmingly well, but Ellen disagreed. She was disturbed that I was barely sleeping. She understood that without accepting new patients a medical practice would dwindle. She noticed I had some difficulty with my vision, and when she asked me about it I explained that my vision was worsening, which was not unusual considering my age, and I said I was happy about it. Ellen found this particular comment disturbing and I tried to explain it to her, but I knew she could never understand.

My vision was becoming such that I could only see things that were between one and three feet in front of me. This was a tremendous relief to me; cutting down on my field of vision meant that there were fewer things that could compete for my attention. This may seem like a high price to pay for improved attention, but it allowed me to focus better than ever, and I needed whatever help I could get. Ellen insisted that I see an ophthalmologist and get glasses. I told her I did not have the time and that it didn't matter because I needed to devote most of my time to teaching Joshua or treating my patients. My vision was more than adequate for that.

Ellen never had to deal with lack of focus in her life. If she had something to do, she just did it. She had no idea how people like Joshua and me had to struggle to keep from being distracted. She also did not understand the concept of hyperfocus, which is the ability of some people with ADD to pay more attention at certain times. Ellen had seen me slip into this before but had never worried about it. I agreed that my hyperfocus was more intense at this point than it had ever been, but under the circumstances it was worth it. I promised her that once I had delineated my theories, I would go and get glasses and have more time for her and Aaron. I told her I was very close to being finished.

I was working furiously.

I was hardly sleeping and I was tired all the time, but there was not much I could do. I reminded Ellen of what she had said: "You will just have to teach him to read faster." But she did not understand what that entailed. What I was trying to do was really difficult.

It required long hours. Like Ellen, I had some doubts about what I was doing and the way I was doing it. I occasionally wondered if I was crazy, but I had come to a conclusion. I had found success, and I had faith in what had brought me this far. I was convinced that I could teach Joshua to read.

chapter ten

Putting Things in Order

Defining Linear and Fragmented Thinking

People's understanding of order is based on information conveyed to them by their senses, that is, what they see and hear. If sensory information is missing, partially blocked, or exaggerated, people must impose order without the benefit of the proper information. Because order is essential for learning, assimilating, and expressing what a person knows, imposing order profoundly affects people's ability to communicate and understand. I was convinced that this was Joshua's problem. I had established in my observations that his sensory input was damaged.

I was also convinced that Joshua's trouble with communicating and understanding was in some way related to the fact that he was blocking, exaggerating, and misfiling sensory information.

The best way I could think to explain it was this: No one wants to sit behind a column at the ballgame because it partially obstructs the view. This affects his or her overall understanding and enjoyment of the game. He or she can observe part of the game and strain his or her neck to see, but sometimes he or she must assess the crowd's reaction and deduce what occurred. This may cause him or her to occasionally miss a play. For the person who watches a game with his or her vision partially obstructed, it will be difficult to communicate or describe in detail what happened at the game.

It was my belief that Joshua had what I refer to as "fragmented thinking," which is akin to sitting behind a pole at a ballgame. He is constantly struggling to understand what is happening without having a direct view. He gets frustrated from the constant strain of only seeing part of what is happening. The people who have direct line of vision I term "linear thinkers." They are lucky to have good seats. They don't struggle to get information, and they have an easier time seeing and understanding what is happening.

People who utilize linear thinking are in the majority and are considered normal. Those with fragmented thinking are considered to be learning disabled. Some people see things backward or see only parts of things. This makes it very difficult to understand one's observations and is responsible for fragmented thinking.

Linear thinking is the process by which information is ordered by how it is experienced and how it is expressed. The thinking process proceeds in a sequential manner, like a straight line.

Most people learn, think, and express themselves in linear fashion. Reading starts at the left and proceeds straight across to the right. In a learning situation, such as a classroom, the teacher speaks while she writes on the board, starting at the left and moving in a straight line to the right. Linear-thinking people find it easy to follow along with her.

Putting things in order is easy and fun for a linear thinker. Things can be put in size order, starting at either the biggest or the smallest, or alphabetical order, or in order of importance, and so on. Order is how things are accomplished. A linear thinker proceeds in an orderly fashion from the beginning to the end to accomplish his or her goal.

Fragmented thinking is the way many people, who are perceived to have learning disabilities, think. They do not move in a straight line. Getting from one place to another efficiently is impossible because they are incapable of going in a straight line. They understand order differently. In fact, the way fragmented thinkers understand order makes the linear thinkers believe that they do not understand order at all. The way they approach the world is comparable to a blind person attempting to do a jigsaw puzzle. They may be able to put the puzzle together piece by piece, but they are at a significant disadvantage because they cannot see the pieces.

They can feel the pieces, though, and may be able to establish a certain order that allows them to complete the puzzle. So they will do it in a different way, in a different order, and probably more slowly than a sighted person.

Some people may need to see or write things from right to left to understand the order, and doing so is like reading a different language, French for example. They many need a translator who can translate their dyslexic vision into a left-to-right orientation. Explaining things to them in a linear fashion does not help; they need a special education teacher who is equipped with special skills. Labeling them as disabled only impedes their progress.

People like my son and I have trouble with order because order is like a language that we do not speak. When it comes to order, we are strangers in a strange land.

Putting this into more concrete terms of a learning situation, a teacher may say:

THE LINEAR THINKER SEES AND HEARS THIS.
Class   take   out   one   pencil   but   not   your   homework.

THE FRAGMENTED THINKER SEES AND HEARS THIS.
Class   pencil   your   homework

The spaces are created by a variety of things that block sensory input: disabilities, inattention or daydreaming (ADD), starting at the wrong end of the board or the word (dyslexia), misinterpreting visual or aural cues, difficulty understanding language, falling off one's seat or dropping a book (ADHD) five times during the sentence, panic, or visceral reactions to certain social situations, such as rejection sensitivity. In our educational system, what would be called endearing idiosyncrasies in an intellectually gifted child are called learning disabilities in a differently abled child.

Finally, armed with this information I was ready to set up a system to teach Joshua a way to learn the difficult letters, taking into account my theory on the basis of order. I needed a way that would de-emphasize linear order, one that would convert hard letters that could be pronounced many ways into a series of easier to remember letters that could be pronounced only one way, and one letter at a time. I hoped that this would enable Joshua to learn his vowels. I got to work.

chapter eleven

Reading and Riding

I was spending only ten hours per week at my office and no longer earning enough money to cover my office expenses. I cashed in my IRAs, one by one, to stay afloat. I didn't tell Ellen because I didn't want her to worry about me. We were fine financially because Ellen had always been the main wage earner. However, I had always loved practicing medicine, and if she realized that my practice had dwindled it would be cause for concern, especially because it was now obvious that I was seriously sleep deprived. I was so tired that I could barely keep my eyes open and I was falling asleep almost anywhere I sat down. Ellen wasn't sure whether to feel sorry for me, be angry with me, or take me to a hospital.

I was awash in scraps of paper and notebooks filled with observations about what Joshua did and did not know, theories about order, personalized definitions of easy and hard, and stories of my past learning triumphs. I had also accumulated an awesome assortment of index cards and dictionaries.

I pasted the "Alphabet Too," now with over sixty letters, all over the house as I kept trying to think of new letters. Ellen was a pretty good sport about this. Joshua could see how many letters he knew and was gaining confidence.

Aaron was about two and a half. He taught himself the alphabet one day when we weren't looking. I found this upsetting. Ellen and I probably should have celebrated Aaron's accomplishment but it was no big deal to him and we were afraid that making too big a thing out of it might embarrass Joshua. I pushed on with my efforts for Joshua and I promised myself I would soon make it up to Aaron in other ways.

Ellen kept urging me to see a psychiatrist because I wasn't sleeping as I toiled obsessively at trying to unlock the secrets of Joshua's mind. I referred to the work as my "Magnificent Obsession." Ellen referred to it as my "Descent Into Madness," and I was pretty sure that she thought that was joke— at least I hoped so. I kept telling her not to worry because I was almost done, and again promised her that I would make sure to turn off the computer at midnight and come to bed. We both knew I was lying.

I decided to compile a simple but unified theory of how to teach Joshua to read. Obviously I would first start with the alphabet except I would use our alphabet.

Constant repetition: It was clear to me from my previous learning experiences and from observing Joshua that constant repetition was essential to the learning process. Practice makes perfect, I kept telling Joshua. But this meant intermittent, brief repetition of bite-size pieces of information from the second he woke up to the second he went to sleep.

Stolen moments and brief encounters: Although continuous brief repetition of mini-lessons of less than two minutes was important, the materials also had to be portable, and the smaller and lighter the better. I could not carry a blackboard with me to a movie theater, but I could carry small business card–sized study notes. Each card could contain a tiny lesson, a letter, or something else that I could whip out standing in line at the movies or in between batters at a baseball game.

The Easy Rider Alphabet: This was our alphabet, the one I had painstakingly been recording and that we had called "Alphabet Too." It would now be called "The Easy Rider Alphabet." It consisted of all the sounds that Joshua knew or I wished he knew in addition to the regular alphabet. We had seventy letters at this point, though we would often add or remove letters depending on how either Joshua or I felt about them at any given time. The alphabet evolved with our needs, devoid of order. I would say, "Let's get the Easy Rider," or "Where is the Easy Rider?" Joshua thought it was great that his alphabet had a name that involved riding because he loved riding in cars even though he fell asleep almost instantly upon getting into one.

THE EASY RIDER ALPHABET

A	EN	L	R
ACE	ENG	M	S
ACK	ESE	N	SH
AI	ET	O	T
ALK	F	OCE	TH
AN	G	OCK	U
ANG	H	OLL	UCK
ASE	I	ON	ULL
AT	ICE	ONG	UN
AY	ICK	OO	UNG
B	IE	OSE	UT
C	IGHT	OT	V
CH	ILL	OU	W
D	IN	OUGHT	WH
E	ING	OULD	X
EA	ION	OW	Y
ECK	ISE	OY	Z
ED	IT	P	
EE	K	PH	
ELL	KN	QU	

Cars: Everything I did would have to be somehow woven into a fabric with a car motif.

Joshua loved cars, and I thought it would make learning more fun for him. He would spend time endlessly arranging them in lines and circles. We bought him a carpet that had a simulated map with roads big enough to put toy cars on. He had books and games that included cars. He understood how cars worked. We went to the Car Show every year at the local convention center, and he loved it.

Joshua understood the concepts of one-way streets, intersections and lights, and so on. I decided to take what I had learned about how Joshua understood letters and the alphabet and make it into a car game. I told Joshua stories about how I learned to drive and the difficulty of confronting intersections and making decisions there. I described what a great deal of experience I needed before I was able to feel comfortable at an intersection, and Joshua understood. He found all this car talk endlessly fascinating.

Easy and Hard: I had a good handle on which letters Joshua thought were easy and which ones were hard. I divided up our Easy Rider Alphabet as follows:

- **Easy letters** were those that could be pronounced only **one way**.

- **Two-way letters** could be pronounced **two ways**.

- **Intersection letters** could be pronounced **more than two ways**.

A one-way letter could be thought of as a one-way street. The two-way letters could be visualized as a two-way street: cars coming and going in two directions. The intersection letters were visualized just like an intersection of streets. It seemed obvious to Joshua that it was the easiest to drive down a one-way street, harder down a two-way street, and even more difficult to negotiate an intersection. Joshua and I got down on the ground, got some cars, and discussed how our letters were just like cars and streets. It was a bit weird but it was fun and he completely understood the concepts.

I made a three-column chart.

The first column contained one-way letters (which included blends because we counted them as letters).

The second column contained two-way letters.

The third column contained intersection letters.

ONE WAY LETTERS

ACE	ILL	OY
ACK	IN	P
ALK	ING	PH
AN	ION	QU
ANG	ISE	R
ASE	IT	S
AT	K	SH
B	KN	T
CH	L	TH
ECK	M	UCK
ED	N	ULL
EE	OCE	UN

ELL	OCK	UNG
EN	OLL	UT
ENG	ON	V
ESE	ONG	W
ET	OO	WH
F	OSE	X
ICE	OT	
ICK	OUGHT	
IGHT	OULD	

TWO-WAY LETTERS

A	G	OW
AI	H	U
AY	I	Z
E	O	

INTERSECTION LETTERS

C	I	OU
D	IE	Y
EA	O	

The one-way letters were no problem. Joshua knew most of them by now. But the vowels and the intersection letters were a real sticking point. I decided to break down the hard letters into a series of easy letters. In car terminology, this meant converting a two-way street into two one-way streets and making simple and steadfast rules on how to deal with intersections. I also felt I needed a standard paradigm that would work for every single letter in our alphabet of two-, three-, four-, or even five-way letters. Different strategies for different letters would be too confusing.

The answer was so obvious and simple I was astonished when I thought of it. The way to learn a letter would be this:

"FIRST YOU SAY_____THEN YOU SAY_____."

First you say it one way, and if that does not sound right, you say it another way. Every single letter becomes either a one-way letter or a series of one-way letters. There are absolutely no choices to consider, or any worrying about how to pronounce a letter. *A* would always be pronounced "ah" first because all of the vowels would always be said with the soft sound first. *Aw*, however, was not an *A*. It was an *aw*. This is what necessitated so many letters in our alphabet. There were more letters to remember, but they were less confusing because there was less sensory data to deal with at one time.

It was comparable to driving a car down a one-way street. You did not have to worry about cars coming at you from the other way because the street only went one way. There would not be as much sensory data to integrate at any one time.

FIRST YOU SAY:_____. If you get to the end of the word and it does not make sense, you start over with THEN YOU SAY_____. It was a slow way to read, but it was easy. It was very easy to explain and illustrate this concept to Joshua with cars on one of our car maps. First the car would go down a one-way street. If that was the wrong way, it would go down another street.

Joshua would look at the letter *a* and say out loud, "FIRST YOU SAY 'AH,' " That is the only thing he had to remember. He did not have to understand how to use *a* in *all*, or *paw*, or *pain*. It would always be said just one way, and that way was "ah." Then, after he finished the word if it did not make sense he would go back and say, "THEN YOU SAY 'AY.' " This increased the importance of context. I made a lot of copies of this paradigm and would fill in whatever letter we were working with.

---

letter

First you say _____

then you say _____

then you say _____

Multiple Perspectives: Considering my own learning past, I believed that teaching from multiple perspectives was important. For instance, I knew that Joshua could occasionally recognize a letter written large but not small and vice versa, or lowercase and not uppercase, so I had to teach both. I also decided to use lots of color and diagrams because it had worked for me when I needed to learn something. Hanging cards and charts on the wall had worked for me in college, so I hung Joshua's letters everywhere in the house. He could sometimes recognize a letter in one font but not another, or on one color of paper and not another, or in the bedroom and not the kitchen. I used index cards in every color, size, and style, and a wide range of colored inks, crayons, and pencils. Following is an example of how we learned the letter s from multiple perspectives:

S s S **S** s S s *S*

No judgments: There would be no order, time constraints, or pressure of any kind. If he failed I would let him know that it was my lack in teaching and not his in learning. No matter what happened I would make sure that Joshua knew that I loved him and was proud to be his daddy. There would be no failure.

I had a place to start—with the easy letters, and I knew what order to go in. I set out to define a unifying concept by making lots of charts and diagrams.

READING & RIDING

ONE-WAY LETTERS

A prime example of a one-way letter is *s* because it always sounds the same. From our newly named "Reading and Riding Alphabet" we knew that. We also knew that *sh* wasn't really an *s*. It might look like an *s*, but it was a different letter. Just like kids look like their parents, but they are different people. *S* and *sh* were both easy letters because they could only be said one way but they were different letters. Joshua understood this. I had lots of teaching aids for *S* that I had made when we were making our alphabet but I made some more.

S

ssssSSSSSSS**SSS**sSss
SSsSSS**S**sss

THE REALLY TERRIFIC THING ABOUT S

IS THAT IT ALWAYS Sounds THE SAME.

IT SOUNDS THE SAME AT THE BEGINNING OF A

WORD AS IT DOES AT THE END OF THE WORD

BECAUSE IT IS A *ONE-WAY LETTER*.

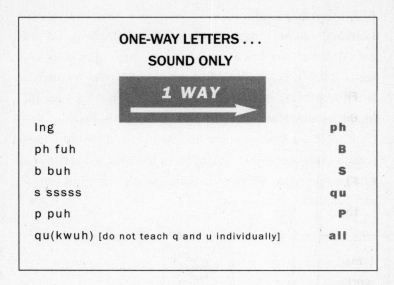

ONE-WAY LETTERS . . .
SOUND ONLY

1 WAY

lng	ph
ph fuh	B
b buh	s
s sssss	qu
p puh	P
qu(kwuh) [do not teach q and u individually]	all

Teaching two-way letters would be the first and most important test of the system. Vowels were a constant irritant—until now. Once I made them two one-way letters it became a lot easier to begin to teach them to Joshua. I realized that the vowels were often pronounced in more than two ways, but I figured I would address that later. I also hoped that that I could handle the varied pronounciations in the same way as the *s* and *sh*, where making *sh* a letter in our alphabet obviated the need of explaining that an *s* sounds differently when it appears with the *h*. I was desperate to teach to him the vowels. I made new flashcards. The vowels were a special case so I grouped them together.

VOWELS

First you say *short*

then you say *long*

First you say _____

then you say _____

a e i o u

SHORT

a e i o u

LONG

I made up cards for all of the vowel sounds, and they worked. I was overwhelmed with excitement, and so was Joshua. We were on a roll. We were going faster and faster as Joshua become more used to the method. He was learning letters like crazy. He could read, very slowly, but he could read. We were both giddy from our good fortune. We were laughing all over the place. It only took about a week to learn the vowels and before we moved on to true intersection letters I made a chart of vowel blends, which we

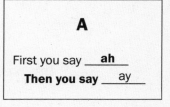

A

First you say _____ah_____

Then you say _____ay_____

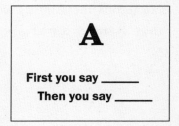

A

First you say _____

Then you say _____

called speed vowels because these letters were pronounced just like vowels but had certain consonants after them and were very common.

I made up a chart of "speed vowels" that merely highlighted what we had learned about vowels and provided practice.

SPEED VOWELS

	N	T	ST
A	an	at	ast
E	en	et	est
I	in	it	ist
O	on	ot	ost
U	un	ut	ust

Intersection Letters

Intersections are representative of the way that Joshua would have to deal with certain words. An intersection letter is to Joshua the same as an intersection is to a beginning driver. It strikes fear and panic into his heart.

AN *INTERSECTION* LETTER,

ed

First you say *tuh*

then you say *duh*

then you say *ed*

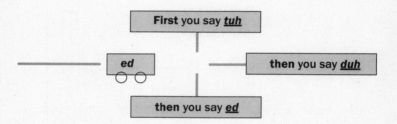

First you say *tuh*

ed

then you say *duh*

then you say *ed*

---

ed

First you say **t**

then you say **d**

then you say **ed**

How do you say it?

1.

2.

3.

ed

The two-way letters were much easier, but they were done in the same way:

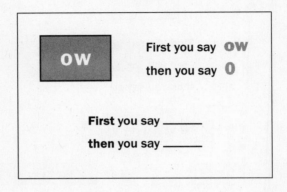

An example of a very easy three-letter word that contains two one-way letters and an intersection letter (said the first way):

Picked

P ick ed

The cornerstone of learning all the future letters of any difficulty was this general paradigm of breaking down a letter that could be pronounced in a variety of ways into a clearly delineated series of easier to remember one-way letters. I put all of our letters into this paradigm and quizzed Joshua on them.

Rules of Reading a Word

I needed to define a few rules on how to read a word as an entity, instead of just letters. I wanted there to be as few rules as possible because I felt that Joshua would have to use these rules every time he read a word, and too many rules would slow him down. I chose my most important three and referred to them as ROR (pronounced *roar*). Joshua liked lions and thought it was a terrific idea. So when he started to read a word and was having trouble I would just say "ROR like a lion." He liked to roar like one.

Rules **O**f **R**eading (a word)

- FIRST LETTER

- FIRST RULE

- S

First letter: This rule helped Joshua remember where to begin. Actually the most complicated rule for Joshua. Not only did he have to read the first letter of a word, he also had to figure out which one it was. This was not an easy task for him. Many people assume that a person will know to start reading at the top of the page, on the left side, and at the beginning of a word. Joshua did not quite understand that. He would often start in the middle of a page and in the middle of a word and then go up or down or across. He also had a tendency to go from right to left and then would often read backwards. Joshua had to learn to find the first letter. In order to do that, he had to find the beginning of the page, and the beginning of the word. By focusing on finding the first letter, Joshua was able to find the right place to start but didn't have to worry yet about pronouncing the whole word. We were taking it one step at a time.

First Rule: Look for the letter *e*. This rule was essential because it freed Joshua from trying to decide how to say vowels in the context of a word. Without this rule, Joshua would often look at a word and freeze. Of course he could use his "first you say_____then you say_____" technique, but it occurs so often that it would really interfere with his reading. By looking for the *e* (sometimes known as the magic *e* be-

---

FIRST RULE

Look for the **e**

The **e** tells you how to say a vowel in a word even though it often comes at the end or in the middle of the word. It is not a letter because it is silent. It immediately simplifies the reading of a word by subtracting one letter and telling how to say another. Two letters is a lot, especially in a three-letter word such as **ate**.

Always say the long sound when you see this e.

cause of the way it changes the way a vowel is pronounced), Joshua would know how to say the vowel in the word. *E* made the vowels sound long, or sound like their names.

S was the last rule. I chose this because Joshua would often forget whatever was at the end of anything: eating, talking, getting dressed, and so on. Even when he learned to read a word he would just miss the *s* at the end. He could look straight at it and not see it. This rule forced him to pay attention to the end of the word and not forget the last letter.

My goal was to teach Joshua to read a word by finding the first letter and then looking for an *e* to see how to say the first vowel and then looking to see if the last letter was an *s*. It was not fast, and I did not even consider it a good way to read, but it was simply Joshua's way. The biggest problem was that it was very slow, so I began to look for ways to speed up the process. That's when we really got into "Speed Vowels." (see page 170)

As time went on, I developed an addition to the First Rule to help Joshua with the troublesome letter *c*.

First Rule Plus C: Next look for the letter *c* with the e. This is more of an extension of the first rule because it was similar to looking for the "magic *e*." The difference was that it involved a *c*. It decreased the possibilities of pronunciation, was easy to spot, and was just like the first rule. I also liked that it included the letter *c*. I thought this was a good opportunity to get around *c*, a letter with which Joshua had so much trouble. When *e* follows *c*, makes a sound like *s*.

FIRST RULE + C=

_ce

Ace	pace	price
Ice	dice	trace
pace	race	slice
slice	lice	Bruce
face	vase	trace
mice	nice	truce
lace	spice	spice
rice	space	spruce

We had a system, but we also had to deal with Joshua's particular challenges to learning.

Attentional Hyperspace and Attentional Gratification

"Attentional Hyperspace" is a term I use to describe a place to which Joshua would catapult at any given moment as the result of certain triggering events. Reading a difficult word would do this. He would get frustrated and suddenly he would launch to that faraway place. I could see it in his eyes. He could not refocus and continue, and there was no way to get him back any time soon.

Rather than overwhelming him with information or material that stopped his ability to focus, I wanted to create a technique that would draw him into a place where his attention would be focused. I felt that I could do this by doing the exact opposite of what caused him to be catapulted into Attentional Hyperspace. I would bring him to "Attentional Hyperfocus," like a magnet draws steel. I would create an oasis in the midst of reading where he could rest and refuel, where, instead of frustration, he felt gratification. This place would be called "Attentional Gratification." On a page full of confusing and difficult words, Joshua could rest on just one word that he could say automatically without thinking.

Certain words were notorious for hurling Joshua into Attentional Hyperspace. I found these words by looking at children's books and finding a word that appeared many times, and which I knew had given him problems in the past. The words had to be common and not easily read with our strategies. I would teach him the word before we read the book. Here I was engaging the crudest form of rote memory. Joshua didn't have to understand the words, just memorize them, even if it took a week. I decided to call them "Week Words."

Choosing the first Week Words was simple. I picked up a few of Joshua's books and a page of a newspaper and scanned them into my word processor. I simply clicked a few buttons and I had the most common and difficult words on the page. In order to be truly scientific I would have had to include a much larger sample, but this was good enough for us. The first Week Word was easy to choose. It was *said*. Joshua had lots of trouble with this word, but to this day he knows the word *said* better than any other word. After just five of these Week Words, Joshua's reading dramatically improved. The five that he mastered follow:

1. you

2. said

3. some

4. would

5. they

I used all of the tricks I had learned so far to enable Joshua to learn. I created study cards, and charts and so on. Following are some representative examples.

said

SaidSAIDsaidSAID

sadsidsaidsiadsaad

SADsaidSIDSAID

SDISSADSAIDsaid

saidsaidSAIDsidsad

dasidaddsaidsads

dasaidasdidadasaid

sssaaasaidiiisssaaa

*saidsaidsaidsaid*saidsaidsaidsai
d

said~said~saidsaidsaid

I said.

You said.

He said

we said.

who said

what was said

I made study cards by purchasing Avery blank business card sheets from the local Staples and printing them up. These were especially good for pulling out while waiting on line at a movie theatre or other event.

said	said
said	said
said	said
said	said
said	**said**
said	said

There were some very easy words that because of their size alone would intimidate and frustrate Joshua. One such word was *attention*. I broke it down for him.

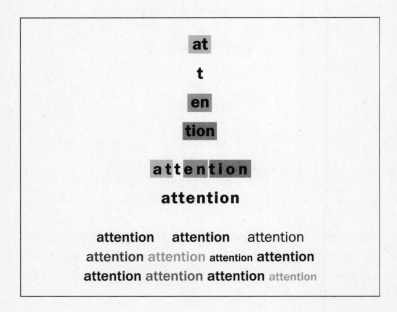

Another word was *interested*:

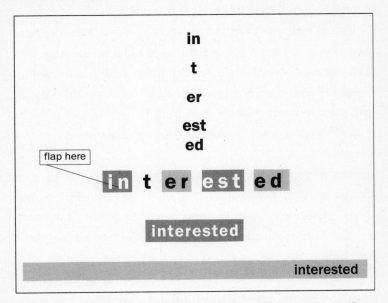

These words did not teach any specific lesson, but they helped Joshua understand that *all* words were easy. One of the ways that I chose these words was to have Joshua look at a newspaper. I would say to him, "What do you think is the hardest word?" Joshua would usually pick out a long word, such as *attention*. I would then make a lesson out of it, and when we were finished we would kid around, saying,

"Oh, that word is really easy." Joshua would go and tell Ellen, "Dad," (he meant Mom), "Do you want to hear a really easy word?"

Ellen would say, "Yes."

And he would say, *"Attention."*

Ellen would say "No, no, no, that's a very hard word. A young boy could never know that word."

Joshua's face would light up and he would show her how easy it was to read the word *attention*. Ellen would gasp and look amazed, and Joshua would laugh really hard. Sometimes we would all laugh really hard. Aaron would come in and start to laugh just for the fun of it.

Joshua would say to Aaron, "Aaron, *attention* is a really easy word."

Aaron would look at his big brother, and I could see him thinking, "Boy, my brother is a smart guy." Joshua would hug him and say, "Don't worry, I will teach you all the easy words when you are big, like me." And we all just kept laughing.

I knew then that I had my family back. I was determined to not lose them again. I was fulfilling a promise I had made to myself a long time ago. Joshua was not going to live my life. My family was not going to live the kind of life my family did when I was a child.

But it wasn't over yet.

chapter twelve

Poetry in Motion

One day I could see that Joshua was worried, and I asked him what was wrong.

"A boy in school told me that in first grade kids have to sit at a desk all day." He did not have to say any more. Sitting still in one place for any length of time was terrifying to both of us.

That was when I realized that I was going to have to teach Joshua in short bursts and stolen moments: before he went to sleep at night, when he woke up, in the car, on the way to school, and standing in line at the movies or the supermarket. They added up to only a few minutes each day, but were very effective because the sessions were short, to the point, and constant. I was relentless. But things change.

Joshua grew weary of learning new letters, especially

since he now believed he could read. I couldn't blame him. After all, he had worked hard and succeeded. His sense of accomplishment was in many ways wonderful. On the other hand, though, I was distressed that he no longer wanted to work on what I considered to be a very important issue: the last few difficult letters. I had to find something new and special that would reignite his enthusiasm.

I considered these last letters my final obstacle. Ellen felt differently. She was happy that Joshua could read, and thrilled that things were straightening out and returning to normal. We were having fun again as a family. I no longer spoke of enemies or felt angry with Joshua's teachers. I was now more philosophical about the experience. Joshua and I had fought the good fight standing shoulder to shoulder and accomplished something that no one thought we were capable of. Nevertheless, I wanted to finish what I had started.

Ight was very difficult for Joshua. I understood; the *g* and the *h*, with all their turns and squiggles, had always made me uncomfortable, and I always hated that silly dot on top of the I, and the T was easily confused with the *d*. But if Joshua could just see *ight* as one letter, an easy letter, it would become an ongoing source of Attentional Gratification and improve his reading.

One night I was thinking about the letter *ight*. I knew I needed to teach Joshua these letters in a way that made him feel like he was reading, but that also kept his attention and allowed for the constant repetition he needed. Suddenly the answer was obvious. A poem. I would write a poem with as many *ights* in it as I could. I slipped quietly out of bed and moved quickly to the next room and turned on my computer. The next time I looked up it was 5 A.M. An hour later I showed the poem to Joshua. He loved it.

there once was a knight
who hated the light
and he was called
the knight
of the night
then there's the knight
with very bad sight
who was known as
the knight
of the light
the knight
of what's right
tried to set up a fight
between
the knight of the night
and the knight of the light
but
the knight of what's right
was not very bright

since the knight of the night
would not fight in the light
and the knight of the light
would not fight in the night
anyway
how can a fight
decide what is right?

I was struck by Joshua's response to this poem. He seemed mesmerized by the rhymes and also understood the knight poem on a variety of levels: He understood the play on words of *night* and *knight,* and the irony of the cowardly knight of what's right trying to impose his will by setting up a fight between other people. He also understood that a fight is not the way to settle anything.

I was amazed and gratified when we read the poem together, though I only asked him to read the words containing *ight,* while I read the other words. After we were finished I would ask him to read any line that he wanted. He loved that freedom. We could do one line, or two, or more, in whatever order he chose. This gave him a much-appreciated measure of control over his learning and did not stretch his attention span. Soon Joshua became an expert at the letter *ight.* The diet food section at the supermarket was like an *ight* museum, with almost everything saying *light* on it. He would point it out in anything he saw, "Look at that easy word." We used to kid around and I would say, "Joshua is the world's foremost authority on the letter *ight.*" And he was.

I thought that if I could write about ten poems we would be done, but I also decided that I should let Joshua decide. When he stopped enjoying learning with me I would be finished. The next night I wrote another poem.

ai

First you say <u>ay</u>

then you say <u>ai</u> like yeah or air

as I walked down the trail

it started to hail

and I was afraid

for my pet snail

I put my snail

in my pail

and went off to mail

the pail to Gail

Gail lived in Maine

so I sent it by train

a snail in a pail

on the mail train

Gail met the train

in Maine

in the rain

which was good for my
  snail
who was frail from the
  hail
and that is all there is to
explain

I was delighted by how much Joshua enjoyed the poems and surprised at how easily these poems came to me. I loved making rhymes and developed a real affection for my rhyming dictionaries.

Next, I decided to work on Joshua's biggest letter problem: "*g*". He just could not learn this by using the "first you say_____, then you say_____" rule. I went to work on my most ambitious poem to date: "Marge the Large Singing Pig." I thought that if Joshua's attention held out for just one more letter it should be this one. The sound of the letter *g*: When it had an *e* after it, it was *juh* but otherwise it could be *guh*. The poem was evocative and repetitive and silly, and I was once again writing all night. "Marge the Large Singing Pig" turned out to be quite a bit tougher than the first two. When I was done, however, Joshua loved it and he knew how to distinguish the *g*, *ge*.

Marge

the large

singing pig

got a gig

at a lodge

above the garage

of a college

singing

a hodgepodge

of knowledge

she was sage

as she sang

from the stage

with a twang

her leg on a log

she sang like a frog

when in came a fog

worse than a smog

it was hard to judge

the edge of the stage

when she felt a nudge

and flew into a rage

she tried not to budge

or plunge from the stage

but her large orange cage

started to nudge

her toward the edge
of the ledge of the stage

as she fell from the log
she tried to snag
her cage through the fog
she felt the stage sag
and lunged for her bag
but she slipped
off the ledge
of the lodge garage
and plunged in a rage
with her large orange cage
from the edge of the stage

I petitioned Ellen for a curfew-free three months to write
the rest of the poems. She agreed on the condition that I see
a psychiatrist about my all-night sessions. I thought it was
somewhat unfair in light of the fact that things had been
improving, but Ellen was still worried and I saw no harm in
it. When he interviewed Ellen and me he asked me what I
would think of a patient who stayed up all night writing
poems about singing pigs and pet snails and who believed
that this was a new reading method. He gave me a prescription for lithium (for manic depression). I filled it, put in the
closet, and threw it in the garbage a few weeks later without
ever taking any. He also gave me a prescription for Traza-
done to help me sleep, but it made me too sleepy to work

so the pills were quickly discarded. Later I faxed the psychiatrist "Dicky Duck" and a few other poems, and he said he thought they were brilliant.

Over the next few weeks, I wrote "Dicky Duck needs a Pickup Truck," "Pies and Fries," "Aws and Ows and Talking Cows," and many others. Joshua was thrilled, and the poems helped us slay numerous reading dragons.

"Dicky Duck Needs A Pick Up Truck" is a poem with evocative, funny characters in silly situations discreetly blended with repetition of *ick, ack, uck, eck* and *ock*.

There *is*, after all, some medical research to suggest that constant repetition either creates neural pathways or reinforces existent pathways in much the same way as a stream of water causes erosion.

A Few Words About CK

The combination that these letters make when preceded by vowels is one of the great *READING SHORTCUTS* of all time. These combinations, when viewed as a single entity (a letter, if you will), replace many arduous and confusing reading steps with *one* simple step.

The letters *i c k* are always pronounced the same—"ick," as in *sick*. On the other hand, consider the possibilities when looking at each letter individually. *I* can be said as "ih," "eye," "eh" or "ee." The *c* can be like "s" or "cuh" or "chuh" as in *chop*.

Dicky Duck Needs A Pickup Truck

I am stuck in the muck, quacked Dicky Duck
I need a big stick or a duck pickup truck
Quack quack I'll just call Buck to send me a truck

But a truck costs a buck and I'm out of luck
I stuck my buck in a sack at the back of my pack
And my pack is back by the clock on deck of the dock
Where I last saw my flock

I just turned my neck for a lick and a peck
And my flock flew quick and were gone in one lick
And did not see me stick in this yucky ick on the deck of
   this wreck

I know that my flock will come back to the dock
When Knack Knock and Knick miss their pal Dick
But for now I am stuck in this ick with no buck to call Buck
for a duck pickup truck

Wait, what this in my sock? Could it be a buck?
The buck that I stuck in my sock for bad luck
Oh what luck, that this cluck of a duck
Put a duck buck in his sock
Now I can call Buck for a duck pickup truck

Hello, Buck, this is Dick Duck
I am stuck in some muck
On the deck of a wreck
Could you send a duck pickup truck?
Quick

Sure, Dicky Duck, I'll get my duck pick up truck
And get you unstuck from the deck of that wreck
One buck to the shack and two to the dock

I have a one-buck that I stuck in my sock
For bad luck so I'll just go to the shack
And walk to the dock, it's only a block
Just send that truck quick

Yes sir, Mr. Duck
I'll be there in a lick and a peck
Just wait on the deck

Lick and peck
Lick and peck
That's what ducks do when they're stuck on a wreck

Joshua had learned a lot from me and I was proud to find that I had learned some things from him. Joshua had been my partner in what we accomplished, but through it all he had still managed to love his teachers and even thought the Learning Specialist was great. Working with him I exorcised my own demons, freeing myself of anger and resentment. My childhood suffering now seemed like a small price to pay for this journey of the heart and mind, taken with my son. I was at last at peace with myself and with those who had inadvertently tormented my son and me.

Joshua could learn, if taught with innovative strategies and lots of patience. He was doing better at school, and even his teachers were impressed. My new attitude improved my relationship with school officials. I spoke with the assistant principal, the principal, and the school director. They were more receptive to what I had to say, possibly because it was said without anger.

But just when Ellen and I were thinking that maybe this school was the right place for Joshua after all, a patient of mine spoke enthusiastically about an institution called The Gateway School, calling it one of the first and finest schools for learning disabled children in the world.

chapter thirteen

A New School

Linda Watrous, a patient of mine who is deeply religious and a teacher, had been a tremendous source of support to me throughout my ordeal with Joshua. As a compassionate person, she sympathized with my heartache for my son; as a patient she understood about the fire in my belly to find answers, and as a teacher she encouraged me to follow my heart in search of my own answers for Joshua.

As a teacher she also understood the educational system. She worked with many of the children who had been dismissed or forgotten by schools and teachers. She believed that there were answers to be found in how to teach these children, and she understood that the way to find those answers was through the love and determination of people with the resources to seek them. The children she worked with often did not have the resources my son and I had. There was often no one who could fight for them. So Linda thought it was terrific that I was looking for a way to teach Joshua to read. I would occasionally impose on her and show her some of the reading lessons I was working on for Joshua. She was always generous with her professional opinion and never shy about making suggestions. I was very appreciative, so it was only natural that I would tell her how well things were going.

One day Linda said something to me that would radically alter the course of my life. She mentioned The Gateway School, one of the nation's earliest and finest schools for children with learning disabilities, which was in New York City but of which I had never heard.

Linda had always given me good advice, so I called Ellen immediately. She was somewhat put off by the fact that I was still speaking to patients about Joshua, and was somewhat resistant, but she agreed to make some calls. Ellen called The Gateway School. To our dismay we found that there were no openings; however, Dr. Davida Sherwood, the director of The Gateway School, told her that one child might drop out of the school and that she would call back in forty-eight hours to let us know if there was any possibility that Joshua could be admitted.

Two days later Dr. Sherwood called and said that one space was open, but she wanted us to understand that Joshua would have to be evaluated and that he would be accepted only if they felt that they could help him. She was not making any promises.

Ellen found the thought of applying to a special school for disabled children troubling. She was worried about how the children would look and act. But when we visited The Gateway School we were overwhelmed by the pervasive atmosphere of acceptance and kindness. Everyone seemed to understand what we had been through.

We realized that the spaces at The Gateway School were very limited because there were only thirty-five children in the entire school. This type of exclusivity is not the kind that parents dream of. If your child is accepted here, it means that your child is severely learning disabled.

We set up an interview time for Joshua. The first moments of the interview process for The Gateway School were to be an epiphany for Ellen.

Ms. Pulanco, the Director of Education at The Gateway School, asked Joshua to join with her and some other children in a game of Simon Says. Joshua, as usual, was eager.

Ms. Pulanco had, to say the least, a presence. We had to strain to hear what she said, but felt compelled to do so. Her pronunciation was perfect but exaggerated, and when she looked at me it was as if she and I were the only two people in the world at that moment. I was immediately smitten. Ellen was not. As Joshua happily walked off with Ms. Pulanco, Ellen watched carefully and subtly stole glances at the other children.

Joshua is athletic, fast, well coordinated, and good at Simon Says. After the first round of Simon Says, Ms. Pulanco walked slowly and deliberately over to Ellen, bent over, and whispered, "Did you notice?" Ellen's facial expression betrayed her true feelings. She had absolutely no idea what Ms. Pulanco was talking about. Ms. Pulanco whispered, "Watch his eyes."

The proverbial ton of bricks was about to fall on Ellen's head. Another round of Simon Says began, this time with Ellen's attention riveted on Joshua's eyes. Now Ellen noticed something very peculiar. Just prior to doing as Simon said, Joshua turned his head ever so slightly for an instant to the right or left to observe what the child next to him was doing. Because of his extraordinary athletic ability and quickness, he appeared to be doing well at the game when, in fact, he did not understand a single word Simon was saying. He had fooled everybody.

As Ellen sat in stunned amazement, something happened that convinced her that this was absolutely the appropriate place for Joshua. Ms. Pulanco sat down with Joshua and held up a paper bag and said to him, "Joshua, what do you think I have in this bag?"

Joshua looked her straight in the eye and said, "A banana."

Now it was Ms. Pulanco's turn to be surprised. She said to Joshua, "How do you know it is a banana?"

"Easy," said Joshua, "I can smell it."

Ms. Pulanco started to laugh; so did Ellen, and so did

Joshua. Joshua didn't know why he was laughing, but then he was not a boy to ever pass up an opportunity to laugh. Now it was Ms. Pulanco's turn to be smitten. That moment began the healing of Ellen's broken heart.

Joshua was accepted at The Gateway School, but Ellen still felt the need to discuss the situation with Dr. Turecki. When she called him he told her unequivocally to send Joshua to The Gateway School. Her faith in Dr. Turecki was immense, so this was the last piece of encouragement she needed in making the decision. From that moment on, our lives would be changed forever in ways none of us could ever have anticipated.

Joshua was set to start at The Gateway School when we were informed that the Board Of Education had to certify Joshua as qualified to attend a school for children with learning disabilities. This raised a two-part issue: One, Joshua was not allowed to go on a school bus with other children from his school without the certification, and he very much wanted to. The other issue was a financial one. Gateway is a funded school, which meant that once our local Board of Education certified Joshua he would come under the auspices of The Federal Disabilities Act. His tuition would be paid by the state, and thus save our local Board of Education over twenty thousand dollars per year. We were certainly concerned about the tuition, and we felt it was our civic duty to relieve our local school board of this expense.

We applied to the Board of Education's Committee On Special Education (CSE), a governing body assigned to administer to the needs of the learning disabled. We knew that it could take up to a year for a response, so I wrote out a personal check for nineteen thousand dollars to Gateway. I remember thinking, What are people who do not have this kind of money supposed to do?

A few short weeks later Joshua started at The Gateway School. We were surprised to find that he was in the first class, which was made up of children who were mostly a year younger than Joshua. We immediately spoke to the school director about it and her answer was unusual, if not startling. She said that she wanted Joshua to have the experience of having Ms. Pulanco for a teacher. She said I would soon understand.

Ms. Pulanco made one thing clear to us from the first day. She felt that Joshua's lowered hat brim was a direct measure of his low self-esteem. She predicted that as his self-esteem rose, so would his hat. She declared that her most important task with our son was to raise the brim of his hat. From anyone else I might have found such a declaration odd. But it sounded good when Ms. Pulanco said it. She also had another phrase that we would often hear at The Gateway School: "Each child will meet with success." I had no idea what her statement meant, but it sounded better that anything we had heard before.

Toward the end of the first week I went into Joshua's room in the morning to help him get dressed and was treated to the first of what would be many amazements. Joshua was doing a bad job of tying his shoelaces, but he was doing it. He had never been able to tie his shoelaces before and had stopped trying. Now, I stood frozen as I watched him do it. I asked Joshua how he learned to tie his laces. He answered matter-of-factly that Ms. Pulanco had taught him. He explained that all the kids knew that Ms. Pulanco had a special way of tying shoelaces that was very easy, and that was why she could teach it to him. "Okay," I said. I realized that Ms. Pulanco was the real thing. She was a teacher. As I quietly shared the good news with Ellen, Joshua walked into the kitchen for breakfast. I was sure if I really looked hard I would see that the brim of his hat had risen just a little. Joshua had met with his first success.

At dinner each night Ellen and I would ask Joshua what he did at school that day. "Nothing," he would say. Aaron would tell us about what he was doing at school. I talked about my day and Ellen spoke about hers. I would also ask Joshua every day if he had homework, and every day the answer was the same: "No." After a few weeks I started kidding him by saying he should tell Ms. Pulanco that his daddy wanted homework. Every day after that Joshua would come home and say, "No homework today," and then he would say, "I really want homework, but Ms. Pulanco said I wasn't ready yet." Finally, one day Joshua had a different answer when I asked him if he had homework. He said, "I told Ms. Pulanco that my daddy wanted me to have homework and she said, 'Tell your daddy not to worry and that he will get used to it.' "

We all had a good laugh over that, and she was right: I did

get used to it. Soon after that, Joshua came home brandishing a shiny metallic folder labeled *Homework*. Joshua explained that it was his new homework folder. He was thrilled that Ms. Pulanco had finally found him worthy of homework. "I can't wait to do my homework," he said, and then he went into his room, closed his door, and did his homework. He did the same thing every single night after that.

I was astounded at the ability Ms. Pulanco had to communicate with Joshua. She was able to get and hold his attention in a way that no one ever had before. She had perfected a number of methods to get and keep the attention of all her students. One technique I have personally witnessed on numerous occasions and which I refer to as "The Pulanco Life-or-Death Chin Grip," was particularly effective and the kids seemed to love it. She would lovingly grasp the chin of the child she was speaking to and maintain an iron-clad grip on it. It was impossible for the child to move as she made strong eye contact, emphasizing there is absolutely no possibility of escape. She then delivered her message in a stern but loving whisper. It worked on Joshua, and it would probably work on anybody. All the kids adored Ms. Pulanco, and I knew why: Ms. Pulanco adored all the kids.

As the year progressed, in place of the child who kept his face buried under the brim of a hat we had a wide-eyed curious kid who did not want to miss anything, and who found his hat a hindrance. He once again reminded me of the way he came shooting out of the birth canal, wide-eyed and looking for action. Ellen and I were exhilarated by how well Joshua was doing. When we were invited to a new parents rap session, we couldn't wait. We thought that it would be great fun to sit in a room and swap stories with other parents in the throes of ecstasy.

The meeting was to be moderated by the school psychologist. Like Ms. Pulanco, she was slightly north of middle age, spoke in hushed tones, and had been at the school for a long time. She was very sweet and always had a kind and encouraging word for the kids and their parents. The meeting was held in the school lunchroom, and everyone worked together to form one large table out of a number of small lunch tables. I could tell that this evening was going to be different than I expected. No one was giddy or ecstatic. In fact, no one was even smiling.

The psychologist began the meeting by introducing herself and explaining that she, too, was the parent of a child with learning problems, which she hoped would help put us all at ease. She asked us to introduce ourselves and briefly describe the path that led each of us to The Gateway School.

Ellen and I, thrilled with Joshua's experience at Gateway, sat stunned as each parent revealed the painful circumstances that lead their children to The Gateway School. We related to those painful experiences, but we could not understand the parents' somber tones. Each parent told their story, many sobbing uncontrollably as they related heart-wrenching experiences from other schools. They were also honest about the personal shame they felt at having a child at a school for children with ADD and learning disabilities.

One parent said she felt like she had hit the lottery when her son was accepted at Gateway. Why, I wondered, was she sobbing uncontrollably as she explained how well her son was doing now? Another parent spoke of a son who was prospering at The Gateway School, but she also spoke freely of her shame and disappointment that her son would not be able to go to regular schools. She also mentioned that when her friends found out her son had problems, they stopped returning her calls for play dates.

I was struck by something I had always known but never put into perspective: The entire family of a child with problems suffers in a multitude of ways. The problem often usurps the financial and emotional resources of a family. It is not enough to make an educational intervention. One must also identify and deal with the family consequences of a child with ADD and learning disabilities.

Ellen spoke before I did, and was brief and to the point. Joshua was happy and learning, and she was thrilled. That pretty much summed up my thoughts, but I felt compelled to speak about how I was not ashamed or embarrassed about my son being at a school like Gateway, and how I only wished there had been a school like this for me when I was a child. As I spoke, I realized that I was coming closer and closer to a decision about something that I knew I had to do.

Soon, Joshua's first parent-teacher conference was upon us. Our parent-teacher conferences used to be filled with anger, guilt, and bickering, but now it was embarrassingly pleasant. Instead of facing a "litany of uns" we were treated to a nonstop barrage of compliments from Joshua's teachers. They all thought he was a hard-working and delightful student and were happy to have him in class. After the teachers were done I asked, "Isn't there anything bad you want to tell us about Joshua?" Shrugs all around. We floated home on a cloud.

At about this same time, I began using the strategies and poems that I had developed with Joshua on some of my young patients with reading problems. Additionally, I spoke with some teachers I knew through my practice, and they began using my methods in their classrooms. One teacher at The Gateway School loved them and used them in her class. Another patient, a school district superintendent, suggested that I publish some of my poems for the Board of Education. She even volunteered to call and talk to some other school superintendents about it. I was gratified to receive positive professional feedback on what I had done with Joshua. I was coming closer to the realization and decision that I had to do something to help children whose parents could not write nineteen thousand dollar checks.

My medical practice was flourishing again, Ellen and I were repairing our relationship, Aaron was a star at nursery school. One day when we weren't looking, he taught himself to write. This time we made a big deal out of it because Joshua was better than he had ever been. But there was one more trial we had to endure.

chapter fourteen

Bureaucracy, Again

We had been waiting for a phone call for eight months from Mr. Big, who directed the Committee on Special Education (CSE) for our local school district. He oversaw the evaluations and referrals of all children in our school district with learning disabilities.

We knew that Joshua had what were referred to as learning disabilities. How could we not know? We had been through hours of testing, evaluations, psychiatrists, agonizing meetings with teachers, an expert, a learning specialist, and numerous school administrators. Joshua had been at The Gateway School for almost a year and he was doing great. He was not taking medication. His math and reading skills were improving. He still stammered and had poor organizational skills, but he was improving in these areas as well.

His teachers loved him and thought he was a great student. This transformation had occurred in nine months at Gateway, which was testament to, and part of, the miracle.

Mr. Big explained that the Committee on Special Education had to do its own evaluation in order to classify Joshua as learning disabled. He confirmed the time, date, and location of the evaluation and said it would take most of the day to do the testing, evaluations, and interviews.

On the appointed day Joshua insisted on getting dressed up and wearing a tie. We decided to walk to the appointment and, as we strolled down the street, Joshua walked, ran, jumped, played air guitar, shot imaginary baskets, scaled walls, and touched everything he could reach as he literally ran circles around us. Suddenly we arrived at the address, which was a hodge-podge of buildings of concrete and metal, with what appeared to be a small loading dock in the middle.

The gates were up, so we walked up to a window and I hoisted Joshua up as we both peered in and Joshua knocked. A security guard came to the window, saw us, unlocked three locks, opened the door a crack, and asked if he could help us. Ellen explained that our son was scheduled for a full day of evaluations and interviews here at the CSE. He glanced at Joshua, nodded, and said he would check and come right back. When he returned he told us, "You must be at the wrong address or have the wrong day or something because nobody here knows anything about you."

"Is this the Committee on Special Education?" I asked.

"Yes."

"Is there a Mr. Big here?"

"Yes, he is the director."

"He called our house and told us to meet him at this address at this time."

"Well, okay, you can come in, but you don't have an appointment. You can check for yourself if you want."

We followed him in and he motioned for us to sit down on some chairs against the wall.

"Are you a policeman?" Joshua asked him.

"No, I'm security guard."

"How come you're wearing a costume?"

The security guard smiled, winked, and motioned to Joshua to keep mum.

As we took our seats we noticed three desks in very close proximity. The guard walked over to the closest desk, behind which sat a female security guard. He bent down and whispered in her ear. She nodded her head yes.

Her desk was immaculate and barren, except for a thin black loose-leaf notebook. After about ten minutes, she gestured to us to approach the desk, which we did. She asked us if we had an appointment.

"Yes," we replied in unison.

She reached to the far end of the desk and laboriously pulled the notebook to her. She opened it to reveal one single page of paper with about twenty hand-drawn lines, and something written on two of them. She looked up at us and said, "I'm sorry, you do not have an appointment." Ellen patiently explained about our appointment. The guard nodded and asked her to spell Joshua's last name. Ellen wrote it down for her and we all watched intently as the guard painstakingly copied the name onto the third line of the lone piece of paper in the black loose-leaf book.

Joshua, clearly enjoying this slow-paced drama, had noisily fallen off his chair about fifty times, and we were relieved to note that no one seemed bothered by the ruckus he was making. Ellen and I sat quietly, watching the guard arrange and rearrange the loose-leaf book to her satisfaction on the desk for about ten minutes. Then she suddenly stood up, carefully removed the page, carried it slowly to the next desk, and waited patiently to be recognized.

The person at the second desk did not wear a uniform. Her desktop had nothing on it, except a multi-line telephone on which she was involved in a loud personal conversation while simultaneously chewing gum. She acknowledged the guard, took the sheet of paper, and gestured to her to please wait just a moment. Finally she got off the phone and carefully studied the page. After a half minute of discussion, the guard nodded and returned to her desk and sat down. The woman at the second desk motioned for us to approach, and when we did she told us that we did not have an appointment. We told her we did. She turned around and looked at the security guard and shrugged her shoulders. We sat down again.

She then handed the paper to an older woman at yet another desk who was deeply involved in filing her nails. The stately lady acknowledged her receipt of the paper with a head gesture and then returned to her nails. After a big sigh, she gestured for us to approach. We did. She told us that she thought that there was some mistake because we did not have an appointment; she wondered aloud if we had the wrong address or time. Ellen pointed out that was impossible because she had received a letter and spoken to Mr. Big, who had called our home and given us this address and time. She turned, picked up the phone, and we returned to our seats.

Suddenly a head jutted out from around the corner of the wall we were sitting against and said, "Are you the Rosemans?"

"Yes," we all answered.

"I think you have made a mistake, you do not have an appointment."

Ellen repeated the story, but this time she added, "We would be willing to come back at another time if we could just have an official document showing that we were here." The woman sighed and said, "I'm the only one here, so I guess I will have to do it myself. I hate it when he does this to me." Then she abruptly disappeared.

Five minutes later a pleasant young woman emerged from behind the wall and explained that she would be testing Joshua and that we should speak to the social worker.

The tester took Joshua's hand and they walked off down the hall with us in tow. She pointed us toward the social worker's office and then continued on with Joshua.

We sat down on the two wooden chairs in front of the social worker's desk. She smiled as she spread our file before her. We were relieved to see that we *had* a file. She asked us to tell her a little about Joshua and we did. Then she discussed her daughter, who was in college. We tried to be polite, and pleasantly passed the time. After our meeting we returned to our seats and waited for Joshua.

Soon enough, Joshua came bouncing out of the room holding hands with the tester. He was in a great mood, and when I asked him how it went he said, "Great, could I come back again?" The tester was very pleasant and told us that Joshua was a delightful child and fun to test. I asked if I could go over the test results with her and we headed off toward her office as Joshua and Ellen left for lunch. She clearly explained her testing procedure and the tests. She noted that Joshua was dyslexic and had some other serious learning disabilities, and probably ADHD. She said that we were very lucky to have him in The Gateway School, where they could address his needs. "Oh, and one other thing," she said as I was leaving. "I would like him to come back to be evaluated by the physical therapist because I detected some proximal muscle weakness." I said okay and returned to my seat in the waiting area. Ellen and Joshua had returned from lunch and Joshua was thrilled to hear that he would be coming back again. We seemed to be the only people there. In fact, we had not seen any other people at all since we had arrived.

Soon another woman approached us and identified herself as the psychologist. Joshua took to her immediately, and as they walked off she turned back and said "This will take about two hours, so you can go out for a while." We decided to stay. About an hour later they returned. Joshua remarked, "Boy, that was fun." I asked if I could go over the test with her, and we walked down the hall together.

Her room was big and dominated by a long conference table. She sat down at one end and I sat down at the other. I asked what tests she had given and she told me. When I asked specific questions about the tests, she said that she didn't know much about those things but that she knew how to administer and grade the test. I then asked how Joshua had done. She said his IQ was pretty good and that he seemed to be a happy boy. He was nice and friendly, though she said she found some of his behavior somewhat odd. "What do you mean by that?" I asked.

"When I told him to move in toward the table, he moved out. And when I told him to stand up, he sat down."

I leaned forward, waiting for her to relate this confusion to his disabilities. No explanation was forthcoming, however, so I thanked her and took my leave.

The CSE quickly sent a report to The Gateway School, and Dr. Sherwood called us in to discuss the findings. They seemed to generally reflect the substance of our visit. We were dumbfounded, as was Dr. Sherwood, that they had found a physical problem in Joshua, who was generally a superb athlete. The Gateway School had not noticed any problem, nor had Joshua's doctor, and nor had I. We thought it was an unnecessary waste of money for the Board of Education to insist on physical therapy for the problem, but were immediately informed that it was not wise to disagree with the Board of Education.

Ellen called a lawyer because she wanted to be sure that everything be done correctly. He told her that he would take care of everything. A few weeks later we received a call from a woman at the CSE to schedule our next visit, which we assumed was to pick up some paperwork the lawyer had mentioned to Ellen. This time we were met promptly by the woman who had made our appointment, and she whisked us right in. We were surprised and appreciative to find that everything was going smoothly this time.

We were led into a small room with three people sitting around a table. They all stood up to greet us, identified themselves, and related their backgrounds and their roles. The woman who had brought us in was the tester and seemed to be in charge. To her right sat a psychologist who was pleasant, well dressed, and kind. To the right of the psychologist was a helpful social worker. To the side and in the corner was a much older woman, a parent wearing a bad wig who nodded at us.

The tester opened a file and took out some typed pages, which we recognized as Joshua's evaluation letter. She said, "I am going to read the evaluation of the tester." Ellen told her that we had a copy and that we had already read and discussed them with the school, so it was not necessary for her to read them to us. The tester replied, "I will read them now because that is the way it is done around here." She began to read the three single-spaced pages clearly and slowly. The social worker and the psychologist occasionally nodded in agreement, and when she was finished the psychologist read the letter written by the other psychologist. When she was done the social worker read the letter written by the other social worker. We had been there for a couple of hours, and finally the tester said, "After a careful review I cannot certify Joshua to stay at The Gateway School. You can leave him there until the end of tomorrow, but he must be moved on Monday. I will assign him to another school as an MIS 4. This classification refers to a type of class where there are fewer children, and is meant for those who are learning disabled. I will also certify him for physical therapy for his muscle weakness."

Ellen and I looked at each other. She asked if we had any questions. I did. I explained that I could not understand how a person who had never met our son could make an evaluation of him. Not only that, I explained that he had been at Gateway for almost the entire year, and that it would be cruel to pull him out with two days' notice and put him somewhere else for the last three weeks of the year. I also mentioned that the actual tester had told me that she thought that Joshua was appropriate for The Gateway School. "Can you explain any of this?" I asked.

"Oh, that tester, what an asshole," she said. "She must have been in a good mood that day. She is always impossible. She fights with everybody. And whatever she told you does not matter because she did not write it down. In any case, I make the final decision. I would not trust anything she had to say."

I began to respond when Ellen kicked my ankle so hard I momentarily lost my breath. She then interrupted and said sweetly, "I was under the impression that we were coming in to pick up our certification letter."

"I don't know anything about it. But I will check. In the meantime let me have somebody explain your rights to you."

I thought to myself, my rights? Was I being arrested for something?

As she left the room, another person came in and read from a clipboard, the substance of which was as follows:

"Do you speak English?"

"Yes."

"Do you understand what has been said?"

"Yes."

"You have been assigned to PS 9, and you must report to school on Monday. If you do not like it, you are entitled to turn it down and will be offered two more options. If you do not accept these options you will simply be assigned unless you choose to seek education privately. Do you understand?"

"Yes."

"Sign here at the X."

Ellen signed.

The tester returned and explained that she had checked and that no one knew anything. She said, "But then you people always think like that if you don't get what you want."

I stood open-mouthed as I pondered her last comment. What did she mean by "you people?" Ellen said, "Our lawyer mentioned that he spoke to Mr. Big and that we were here to sign some papers."

"Oh? Who is your lawyer?"

"Neal Rosenberg."

I did not hear an explosion or see anybody fleeing. I did, however, feel a cosmic shift. The tester, the social worker, and the psychologist were all visibly shaken.

"Is there a problem here?" I asked.

"Oh not for you, but it is a headache for us," the social worker replied.

"Well, there is some friction, but he is a good lawyer for you," said the psychologist.

"I am so glad you didn't bring him with you. I can't stand him," chimed in the tester as she grabbed the form out of Ellen's hand, bent over the table, signed her name, and said, "I just want your file off my desk. I certified your son for two years just to get you out of my district. I never want to see you again!"

The psychologist and social worker seemed embarrassed by the outburst, but they also appeared to approve the outcome. We considered her temper tantrum outrageously inappropriate and were shocked that it came from a Board of Education official who was responsible for making very serious decisions about children's lives. I prepared to launch into an angry diatribe, but Ellen kicked my ankle again, and dug her nails into my arm and dragged me from the room.

We got a letter about a week later from yet another person at the CSE, informing us that our request for our son to attend a special school had been turned down and that Joshua would have to enroll at PS 9 in a special education class there. Ellen called and spoke with the person who wrote the letter. He was very nice and confessed that he had no idea why we had gotten that letter, even though it was from him. He promised he would look into it and call us back.

He called us back a week later saying that he was sorry to inform us that there had been a mistake and that we were not, in fact, certified for The Gateway School and that we must have been mistaken. Incredulous, Ellen informed him that we were in possession of the certification letter that was signed by the tester, in our presence, with witnesses. He said he would get back to us.

When we spoke to him again, he explained that the real reason that we had been denied had nothing to do with anything that happened, but with the fact that Joshua had not submitted his medical form. We could not understand what a medical form had to do with anything, and no one had ever given us one. Furthermore, no one at The Gateway School had ever heard of that as a reason to deny special education to a child. Ellen called and spoke with Ms. Q, who said, "Oh, yes, that was the reason all right."

"How were we supposed to find out?"

No answer.

Ellen said, "Could I drop one off in two hours?"

"Yes," she said. "And make sure to give it to me personally."

Ellen called me and said we needed to get Joshua out of school and take him to the doctor to have a form signed.

"Wait a minute," I said, "I'm a doctor. Why can't I fill out the form and bring it down personally?"

Ellen said, "You had better call first."

I did, and asked to speak with the biggest shot around. I got the assistant director. She said that it would be okay as long as we were not going to apply for any special services such as physical therapy. I said, "Absolutely not."

She said, "Fine, come on down and give it to me personally."

I arrived at the building at 3:50 and stood on the street and stared at the locked gates A fellow walking down the street wearing a gazillion keys on his belt, the clear badge of a building super, awakened me from my reverie.

"Hey, man, did you want to get in?"

"Yes, but it looks closed."

"Well, I know Ms. Q is still there. Come on, I'll let you in."

He pulled up the gate, unlocked the door, and let me in. It was clear to me that this was the only person at the Board of Education who knew what he was doing. I thanked him profusely and walked in. It wasn't quite 4:00, and the place was deserted. I shouted, "Is anybody here." I heard the clunking of high heels and stood still as the sounds got closer. A nicely dressed, pleasant-looking woman of about my same age identified herself as Ms. Q and said, "Just leave it with me and I will take care of it." I handed her the form and waited for some type of a response. I watched her scan the form. She looked up and said, "What kind of a doctor are you?"

"Family Practitioner," I said.

We had a very pleasant conversation, discussing her family and mine. About fifteen minutes passed and we were now seated. She spoke a lot, and I nodded a lot. She was a nice person and a sympathetic figure. After about forty-five minutes she looked at me and asked, "Is your son doing well at The Gateway School?"

"It is a miracle," I said.

"Yes, I know that it is a wonderful school," she said. "I'll take care of this for you, don't worry."

I was moved by our discussion and I believed her when she said she would take care of everything, but when I got home and told Ellen she said, "Sure, how many times have they told us that?" But I knew. And I was right. We had no more problems with the CSE. Joshua rode the bus the following Monday and for the final weeks of school.

At the next meeting of The Gateway School Parents Association Dr. Sherwood gave the results of the Board of Education's actions. She said that everybody at the school had received certification for the coming year. There was a collective sigh of relief, and she added, "Except the Rosemans. You," she said, looking directly at us with a puzzled look on her face, "have, for some reason, been certified for *two* years. That is very unusual." I knew it was unusual, but I also knew that, as a doctor, I had learned to read hearts. I had believed that Ms. Q would take care of mine, and she did.

chapter fifteen

Life Is Not Only Fun Again, It Is Funny

Life was not only getting to be fun again, but sometimes it was actually funny. The difference was that we could laugh at things that had previously been upsetting.

Each morning I would go into Joshua's room and see him staring blankly at his closet, without a notion of how to proceed. Eventually he became impatient and sought my help.

"Dad, could you tell me what to do?"

"Put your shirt on, then your underpants, then socks, then your pants, and then your shoes. Read the list on the wall, Joshua!"

"Thanks."

After breakfast, when Joshua went into the bathroom, he would often stand in front of the sink, not doing anything in particular. He knew he was supposed to be there but he wasn't really sure why. "Brush your teeth, Joshua, and use toothpaste," Aaron would say. Aaron was really good at brushing his teeth and he always remembered toothpaste. Unfortunately, he often swallowed his toothpaste, but, no one is perfect.

One morning, I remember glancing into the bathroom just to make sure that Joshua was brushing his teeth. He had to stand on the bathtub rim to reach the toothpaste, and that was where he was at that moment. But he was not brushing his teeth. He was urinating into the sink. I said, "Hey Josh, why are you peeing in the sink?"

He said, "Oh, that's right, I meant to brush my teeth."

No further discussion followed, only a chuckle. It reminded me of the time I had urinated in the kitchen garbage can when I was about his age. When I realized what I had done, I was mortified. I rushed to clean it up, hoping no one would notice. I knew that all hell would break loose in my home if my parents found out. It would certainly mean another trip to the shrink. My parents would act hurt and drone on about what good parents they were and about how shocked they were by how bad I was. It would always end the same way—with a wistful, disappointed look as they remarked, almost in unison, "How could you do such a thing to us? What did we do to deserve this?"

Here and now, however, Joshua and I could both laugh at the absurdity of the act of urinating in the sink. I was certainly not going to let Joshua feel mortified about a mistake like that. After all, I notice that some kids litter, tell their parents to shut up, shoplift, or even worse. Joshua would never do any of those things. I could live with an occasional error. Besides, I understood the similarities in form and function between sink and toilet and why it could be confusing for Joshua. What the heck, it *was* funny. Joshua thought it was funny, though he was a little embarrassed. But there would be no trip to the shrink, and he would not have to live in fear that he was crazy. Most important, he did not have to feel like he was a plague to his parents. Aaron was not amused, but he would not cower in his room, trying to figure out why his brother was so horrid. Of course, I suspected that he would surreptitiously scrub the sink with Lysol, but then at least he could shrug his shoulders and say, "Well, that's Joshua. He may not be perfect, but we love him anyway."

And we do.

The vampire story that Joshua was telling was actually pretty good. We could see the organizational strategies that Joshua had learned at Gateway were working. He was able to start the story at the beginning and tell something about the middle and even as he raced to the punchline we were still impressed by his improvement. As he came to the end of the vampire story he said, "And the men were going to

put a stake through his heart and the women were all standing around with their 'pluses.' "

We all started to laugh as we pictured people trying to
kill a vampire with the addition sign instead of the cross. It
is the kind of laugh you get occasionally. "Pluses," we all
kept saying as we rolled around on the floor belly laughing.

"That is really a good one," I said. "What a gift, to be able
to make people laugh in that way."

Joshua thought it was great, too. He didn't feel that we
were laughing at him. He knew we were just laughing at
something funny that he said. I could see the emergence of
a person who was beginning to fall in love with words.

I was shocked when Joshua said he really liked *ET* and
wanted me to buy it for him. Joshua never liked television
or movies. He could not pay attention long enough to watch
anything through to the end. I was even more shocked when
he said that he would be willing to learn to count by three's
up to fifteen to get it.

I moved quickly to my immense supply of neon multicolored index cards to prepare a variety of study sheets and
flashcards. Suddenly from the kitchen I heard the familiar
refrain, "Joshooooooahhh, tie your shooooooehsssss or you
will miss the bus." In desperation I grabbed a card. It was
definitely not one of my better creations, as I couldn't fit all
the numbers in a line down the index card. It looked like
this:

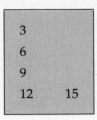

3
6
9
12   15

I thought to myself that Joshua would never be able to go down the row and to the right. The print was bad, the card too small, and the order confusing.

"Hurry up, Dad, I don't want to miss the bus. I need the card," Joshua said. I had no choice. I put it in his pack. As he ran toward the bus he looked over his shoulder and shouted, "Dad, I really want eetee. I love that movie."

"Don't worry," I said, "I will get the movie if you learn the card."

Because I never watch movies I assumed that I could just go to a store to and purchase *E.T.* At the third store I went to, a nice salesperson was kind enough to explain that I was having difficulty because the movie was due to be reissued so there was a dearth of them until it came out. He told me that although he did not have it in stock, he had seen two copies in another video store about thirty minutes away. I asked Ellen if she could get it. We both thought it was a lot of trouble for a movie, but we wanted to let Joshua know that we were ready to reward him in any way for learning. Ellen assured me that she would take care of it.

I left work early and pulled up to the house just as Joshua was getting off the bus. His first words were, "Did you get eetee?"

My wife nodded affirmatively. Joshua, to our delight and amazement, counted by threes to fifteen. Ellen handed him the tape. He looked at the tape and said, "This is not eetee, I wanted eetee."

"This is *E.T.* I ran all over town to get it. Look at it. It says *E.T.*"

"No," said Joshua, "the movie I saw at Corey's house was eetee."

"No," said Ellen, "The movie you saw at Corey's house was eedee."

"Yeah eetee," said Joshua. "That is what I wanted, eetee."

I didn't know whether to laugh or cry. I was thrilled that Joshua had actually wanted something and formulated a plan to get it. It was the old *d/t* thing in a new, surprising, and convoluted way. *Ed* was a children's movie revolving around a baseball-playing chimpanzee named Ed who loves to eat chocolate-covered frozen bananas. We ran out immediately and easily purchased *Ed* and Joshua watched it a few thousand times.

We will be laughing about that one for a long time in my family. Every time I think about it I start to giggle. But it was an important moment: Joshua had acquired a certain confidence while at the Gateway School. He had learned to announce that he wanted to do something hard, and he was able to make a bargain to get it.

•   •   •

When the new Harry Potter book came out, all 732 pages of it, I wasn't surprised that Joshua wanted to wait in a line at Barnes Noble at midnight to purchase it. Joshua and Ellen went and stood on line to get a copy because Joshua just could not wait until the next day. When they returned, I noted that his face was buried in the book as he walked through the door. Ellen insisted that he put the book down and go to sleep because it was almost 2:00 A.M. When I awoke at 6:00 in the morning, I breezed past his room and was surprised to see his light on. I glanced in and noticed that he was reading his new book. I said, "Have you been up all night reading that book?"

"No," he exclaimed. "Mommy said I had to go to sleep last night, but she didn't say I couldn't get up early to read it, so I set my alarm clock for 4:00 A.M."

He's a sly one, that Joshua Roseman.

Two days later I noticed him reading another book and I said, "What's the deal with the Harry Potter book you were so hot to read a couple of days ago? Didn't you like it?" He said, "Yes, I loved it, but I finished it yesterday so I started another book."

Will wonders ever cease? I asked myself. I was proud of Joshua, and I was honored that as a parent I was able to do for him what no one had been able to do for me. But as I thought about that, I realized something. My parents *had* done it for me. Whatever they did, it allowed me to be able to do this for my son. For some reason, that thought always makes me want to cry, and sometimes I do.

Joshua's story does not end here because it is constantly evolving and developing. Learning begins at the first moment of life and continues to the last breath—and so do learning differences. Joshua and I do not have all of the answers but we found some of them. With love and determination, the burden of shame borne by the staggering percentage of people with learning disabilities and Attention Deficit Disorder—a burden that can lead to drug abuse, crime, and dysfunctional family and work lives—can be lifted. That is my belief, my hope, and my expectation.

Music and Flying Dolphins

Joshua wasn't much of a talker, but that didn't stop him from being able to learn from two wonderful teachers who weren't great talkers either. It has become clear to me that the ability to teach can overcome almost any child's perceived learning disability.

When Joshua was five he was studying violin and piano. He liked it for the same reason he likes learning most things: He liked the teacher. But this was a very unusual teacher, which we knew from our initial encounter with him. One muggy afternoon, as Ellen and Joshua were walking to the playground, they literally bumped into a casual acquaintance, a musician known as Dr. Lehman. He took one look at Joshua and with a big smile, a grand gesture, and a certain European charm, beckoned him to, "Come inside and take

a music lesson." Who could resist such an enticing invita-
tion? Certainly not Joshua, even though he had no idea what
a music lesson was.

Dr. Lehman, a graduate of the Moscow Conservatory of
Music, had been a professor of music in his native Russia.
After settling in America, he had performed as a violinist
and taught music, and was now starting a music school for
children. Was he just standing on the street hoping that
someone would walk by so he could invite them in for a
music lesson? It was doubtful, but then, Dr. Lehman made
that improbability seem somehow normal. On that warm,
humid day he wore a light blue, well creased but pleasant
looking suit, and a loud, perfectly Windsor-knotted tie. His
suit fit well, easily containing his slight, wiry, perpetual motion machine of a body. His head bobbed separately to a very
different rhythm, with delicate but well-coiffed hair dangling
from his head and dancing to yet another beat. His air of
competence resulted from the power of his charismatic personality. Dr. Lehman had an endearing way about him, and
his barely contained high energy and good humor were ex-
hilarating and infectious. As he dropped to the ground to
encounter Joshua directly, it was immediately obvious that
he loved interacting with children. From that first moment,
Joshua was crazy about him.

Dr. Lehman could hardly speak English, and what English he *could* speak was barely understandable through his
thick Russian accent. Yet Joshua sat rapt that first day, and

from then on, as Dr. Lehman, gesticulating wildly and apparently out of control, taught him music as if they were playing a game of charades. Dr. Lehman knew that most people had difficulty understanding him, but he did not let that get in his way. He was determined to communicate his love of music to his students in whatever way he could. Joshua, always somewhat puzzled by speech, found pantomime a relief. It was comical, but it worked. Dr. Lehman, a man who had trouble speaking, and Joshua, a boy who had difficulty understanding speech, communicated with each other just fine, constantly ping-ponging musical charades and thoroughly enjoying it.

Joshua eventually lost interest in the violin, and sports began to take up too much time for him to take music lessons. He looked back wistfully on his studies with Dr. Lehman, but as usual, he was on to the next thing. But ping-ponging charades would come up again when the days of the Flying Dolphins were upon us.

Joshua, at eight years old, was doing well in his third year at The Gateway School, but his energy level was still very much an issue. We realized that we had to do *something* to tire him out or *we* would never get any rest.

I confided in a patient of mine about Joshua, and she told me of her young daughter's extraordinary experience on a local swim team. She encouraged me to put Joshua on the team. He enjoyed swimming, and was pretty good at it, so swimming seemed like a good way to burn up his excess energy.

I assumed the team would be a bunch of underachieving kids trying to learn how to swim and get some exercise. I thought that their fathers, who I assumed would escort them in some sort of male bonding ritual, would be a bunch of beeper-wearing guys with big bellies and *Wall Street Journal*s under their arms. Some, I fantasized, would smoke cigars, and others would wear lots of gold jewelry. I did not smoke or wear any jewelry, but was comfortable with my expectations and willing to do it for Joshua. I signed up for tryouts, and remember thinking it was cute that they called it "tryouts."

As soon as Joshua and I walked into "tryouts," I realized that I had been suffering from a gross misapprehension. First, there were hardly any fathers. All I saw were mothers dressed in blazers, fake pearls prominently displayed on well tanned skin, and dark blue or black suede loafers with gold chains taking the place of the pennies in what should have been penny loafers and nobody blinked. As I entered the pool area and listened to the conversation buzzing around me, I had a sinking feeling in my gut. I realized that this was a *real* tryout. I was the *only* overweight dad wearing a beeper.

Dressed in my Hawaiian shirt and Bermuda shorts, with beeper and telephone in hand, I plopped into a space in the tightly packed bleachers overlooking the pool. One empathetic woman was kind enough to include me in the conversation with some of the other blue-blazered mothers.

"Is this the first time your son is trying out for the team?"

"Yes."

"How nice. Where has he been taking lessons?"

"Well, actually a young girl who was a counselor at his day camp last summer gave him a few lessons in her backyard."

They all stared at me without blinking and then in unison shifted their bodies in different directions. It was as if I had been in a huddle on a football field, and the huddle suddenly broke and I was left muttering, "Where did everybody go?"

I was now *very* anxious for Joshua. I was afraid that tryouts would turn into a dreadful and humiliating experience for him. I did not want him to be mortified. I did not want to crush what I perceived to be his delicate ego which his school *and* I had worked so hard to preserve. I *knew* that he was going to have trouble understanding what was going on. After all, *I* had totally missed the point. I felt uncomfortable, and I did not want my son to have those same feelings. But there was nothing I could do. Joshua was already in the water, and the coaches were giving directions. I couldn't yank him out of the water now. My heart was aching.

There were four lanes, each with two coaches and about ten kids. A quick calculation told me that though there were eighty spots to be had, at least one-third of the aspiring swimmers would not make the team. I was relieved, thinking that I could explain to Joshua that he had plenty of company in not making the Flying Dolphins. As I sat marveling at the swimming expertise of the kids, I was reminded of my initial feelings at Joshua's first school. Everything seemed absolutely terrific, and though I doubted that Joshua was going to be accepted, I fantasized about how nice it would be if he were. I was brought back from my reverie by the sound of a whistle.

The coaches asked Joshua to do the backstroke. Whoops, we had forgotten to teach Joshua the backstroke. He did sort of know how to do it—he had to swim on his back, but then the concept of front and back had always eluded Joshua. Joshua tried to do what the coaches asked of him but he could not. He had to stop periodically as he struggled to put two or three strokes together before standing up and trying again. The coaches were very kind and tried to explain to him what to do, but Joshua has problems with instructions under *normal* circumstances. Nevertheless, he kept at it. He would not give up. He really wanted to make the team. It was painful to watch him struggle, but I was proud of him for not giving up.

It was hard for anybody *not* to notice how bad he was doing, and the head coach approached him and patiently explained to him how to do the backstroke. Joshua appeared to listen intently, and on his last few yards, he did something that might be considered a form of backstroke.

Next was the breaststroke. This time Joshua had no idea what they were talking about—all the different movements and the scissors kick confused him. Again, the coaches were in there trying to help him, but he just sort of struggled, doing a modified dog paddle across the pool. Some of the other parents were doing a bad job of not staring at me and showing that they felt sorry for me. But I was proud of Joshua's grit.

Finally came the freestyle. At least Joshua knew how to do that. He had taken those few lessons from his camp counselor, *and* it was clear the boy *loved* the water. They asked him to dive in, another thing he did not know how to do; noting that he was not benefiting from their explanations, they finally just asked him to jump in. Joshua loved jumping into a pool: He did it with pizzazz, and then he took off. He was not much to look at, but he was pretty fast, and had no problem getting across the pool. As he got to the far end of the lane and catapulted himself out of the pool I could see he was proud of himself. I was very proud of him. He had done his best. I thought, "Okay, we learned to read, now I can just get him some swimming lessons." Immediately after the tryouts I went over to the head coach, who had been so nice to Joshua, to inquire about lessons. I could barely understand a word he said because his Spanish accent was so thick, but I could not help but notice his gentle manner: He spoke to the kids in a way that demonstrated that he was a kind and patient soul. He was *exactly* the kind of person I wanted to teach Joshua to swim competitively.

That night the coach himself called. Again, barely able to understand his heavily accented and broken English, I was almost unable to believe that I understood him correctly. Finally I got it. He was saying that Joshua had made the swim team. I was shocked and thrilled. After all, the kid could only do one of the strokes. Nevertheless, for some reason, the coach wanted him. The coach had seen something special in Joshua, and it wasn't his disabilities.

I accompanied Joshua to the first practice session, and once again marveled at the prowess of the other swimmers. It was clear that Joshua would need instruction, and the coach got right to it. Joshua's attention was riveted on the coach for the entire session, and I was convinced that after the two-hour practice his swimming had improved. I was amazed at Joshua's ability to maintain a high level of concentration for that length of time. I had never seen him do that before. As Joshua and I left the building, he looked up at me and asked, "Can I come back tomorrow?" I replied that he could, now that he was on the team. He nodded and was happy, although I realized that he had no idea what this team thing was all about. But he did understand one thing— he could come back again. On the ride home Joshua and I did not say much to each other, but we held hands and I was so happy I felt like crying. Then suddenly Joshua said, "What are we going to do now?"

I had noticed that every other kid on the team was dog-tired after the practice, but not Joshua. He was ready for more, and that was a good thing because you really have to love to swim to be on a competitive swim team—four practice sessions per week, plus meets that sometimes last entire weekends. Joshua didn't say much about it, though he was always happy to go to practice, and *was* rapidly learning to swim at a competitive level.

After a few weeks I noticed a serious problem that I thought related to Joshua's disabilities. Joshua was able to dive into the pool to race, and was routinely beating many of the other kids on the team. Diving was no longer a problem—or so it seemed. I noticed, however, that when the start signal was given, Joshua had to quickly glance over at the swimmer next to him to know when to begin. This put him at an immediate disadvantage, as races are won and lost by fractions of a second. I knew that I had to speak to the head coach about it. I thought that if they could just use the same starting device that they used for other disabled swimmers such as the deaf, it would be better for Josh. I gathered my nerve and went over to speak to the coach.

Cesar, the head coach, had been a Venezuelan champion swimmer as a teenager, but had rejected the harsh coaching prevalent in so many Olympic training programs. He listened to and respected each child, never yelling, as he patiently searched for useful, kind, and encouraging words. He was also big, really big, with long arms and legs responding quickly in concert as he moved about with a graceful athletic gait. He moved as if in a mini ballet, darting around the pool, directing the children. He didn't have rippling muscles or an ounce of fat and it was clear he was a world-class athlete. He was a great swimmer and capable of swimming lengths of the pool effortlessly and quickly. Yet, while he

expressed himself beautifully with his body, expressing himself verbally in English was another story. When he spoke,
the grace and power that emanated from his body simply
abandoned him. He could barely speak English, and what
English he did speak was barely understandable through his
thick accent; however, he gladly repeated himself over and
over each time, adding a little more body English to our
mime-like conversations, until I finally understood him. He
was very patient. Because of this language disability, he had
to speak with his body, and used it constantly as he demonstrated to the kids exactly how he wanted them to kick or
use their hands or dive. He was always in the water dem-
onstrating techniques, unlike many other coaches, who stand
on the side of the pool and bark orders to the swimmers. He
was, in short, a great teacher.

It was obvious early on that Cesar really liked Joshua. He
was thrilled with Joshua's rapidly developing swimming
ability and his attitude. He appreciated the way Joshua always showed up for practice, practiced hard, and listened
intently to his every word. Joshua was also starting to win
races, and coaches like that, too.

In any case, I needed to explain Joshua's diving difficulty
because it was clear to me that nobody else noticed. I took
a deep breath and explained to Cesar how Joshua had some
learning and speech issues. I went on about Simon Says, and
finally finished with my explanation about Joshua's hitch in
his dive: He had to glance over at the other divers to know
when the race started, instead of responding to the starting

signal. I wondered if it were possible to use the same type of apparatus that was used for deaf swimmers. Cesar listened intently, and without hesitation responded. "The one special thing, for me, about Joshua is that he is a child who learns from his mistakes. When I teach him something, he listens and tries not to make that mistake again, and I know he is thinking about it always. For me," he said, "Joshua is a very good learner. I can teach him about the dive."

I thought, This guy doesn't get it. He clearly understood what I was saying, but he failed to understand how teaching Joshua about diving was different from any other teaching problems he faced as a coach. His job was to teach Joshua, and he would. He did not yet know how, but he realized that as a teacher you just have to figure out a way to teach in a way that your student can understand. I suddenly realized how different this was from what Joshua had originally faced in school.

To him, Joshua had no learning *dis*abilities, only learning *a*bilities, and he saw Joshua not as a learning *problem* but merely as a student. He had faith not only in Joshua's ability to learn but in his own ability to teach. That he had never dealt with this before was no big deal to him. I decided to try to figure out why this teacher believed what so many other teachers had categorically denied—that Joshua was a good learner.

At the next swimming practice I carefully watched Joshua and his coach interact. He was correct: Joshua *was* a good learner. Joshua *seemed* to understand him. Every time Cesar showed Joshua how to do something, Joshua understood and did it. Suddenly it was clear. The coach who could not speak was teaching a kid who could not understand speech. The coach, accustomed to people not understanding him, had developed a manner that was very physically expressive. He was very animated, so whatever verbal cues Joshua missed, he was able to pick up by physical cues.

They were absolutely perfect for each other, Joshua and his coach, and they liked each other—the coach who was kind, speaking to the boy who could only learn from a teacher who would *be* kind. The coach adapted his teaching methods until he found a way Josh could understand—quite unlike the way teaching is traditionally approached in schools.

As the season progressed, it was clear that Joshua was becoming one of the best swimmers on the team. The breaststroke, previously a mystery to him, turned out to be his *best* stroke. His freestyle was beautiful, and his backstroke was magnificent. In one race, the two hundred yard freestyle, his level of accomplishment astounded us. He was the only kid from the team entered in that race. He came in last, but he finished, and he was only eight years old. It was clear that soon he would be a star. To me he was already a star. I did not care if he ever won a race.

I stopped worrying about Joshua after that, about whether he would ever be able to hold a job or fit into the non–learning disabled world. Joshua would fit in just fine if he was treated with kindness and not prejudged. He *could* learn.

He just needed to learn differently. Now that he was meeting with success in learning things, he was internalizing the fact that he was a *good* learner and beginning to understand the things that made it easier for him to learn.

At the final awards ceremony, Joshua received a large trophy for the most valuable swimmer in the eight-year-old and under category. It was a great honor because it was a testament to a teacher who overcame a disability and was able to teach, and a student who overcame a disability and was able to learn.

Other Kids Just Like
Me and Joshua

In Joshua's second year at The Gateway School, something happened that shook me to my core. I found out about it in an unusual and disturbing way.

A patient of mine, a board member at the church that housed Gateway, casually mentioned that the church would be expanding its own programs and needed the space it had provided to Gateway. I was neither surprised nor alarmed, but I did find it odd that no one had mentioned it at the school.

Curious about the move and wanting to offer to help, I called the school's Chairman of the Board of Trustees, Ken Plevin. Ken welcomed my call but was surprised by my question because no announcement had been made yet. As he sadly explained the situation, I understood why. The school needed to move, and it was broke.

"So the school will have to close?" I said.

"That is probably true," he answered.

Upset and shaken, I rambled on for a few moments about how much Gateway had meant to my family. Ken was sympathetic and quick to point out that even if Gateway closed it would not be for four years, and Joshua would have graduated by then. I was relieved to hear that, but I was ashamed of my selfishness. What about other kids who were just like Joshua and me? I wondered aloud. Ken said he was planning a meeting of the Board of Trustees and some other people in the hope of saving the school. He said that he would invite me.

In the meantime I began to think about what it would take to move the school. It seemed an impossible task because it was run more like a charity than like a school. The budget was tight, but everyone chipped in where they could. The church charged very little rent. There was no money for substitute teachers so when one was needed, Dr. Sherwood filled in. With no money for lunch monitors and staff, the teachers simply ate with the children. Everybody did extra jobs. The teachers could have made more money elsewhere but they stayed because they loved the children. There were also some extraordinary staffing expenses: physical therapists, occupational therapists, speech therapists, classes of eight children with two teachers, specialized gym teachers, and special music teachers.

The meeting was held in the home of an alumni parent and Ellen and I attended. As I walked in I noticed that everyone was dressed conservatively, and well. I was wearing chinos, a Hawaiian shirt, and sneakers, and felt like I looked like the pizza delivery boy. Feeling a little out of place, I sat quietly for most of the evening as person after person gave testimony to what a blessing the school had been for their children and how sad they were that the school would probably have to close. I was astounded that such a seemingly successful and appreciative crowd could feel so hopeless about the situation.

I assumed that nobody wanted to fight to save a school that they were ashamed their children attended. They were appreciative for the help they received, but they preferred to keep it a secret if they could. Finally I decided that I had to say something. I stood up nervously and slowly, self-conscious about my attire, and took a deep breath.

I said that Gateway needed its own home, and that it would take five million dollars to build it, and that if everyone swallowed their pride and asked everyone they knew for help we could do it. I saw derisive looks and heard sarcastic comments about my lack of understanding of the issues. They may have been correct about my not grasping the difficulty of saving Gateway, but as a person with learning disabilities I had learned to deal with adversity. This was no tougher than teaching Joshua to read.

Once again, I was on fire. I knew I had to do two things: I had to find people to help me who were not so pessimistic, and I had to find people who were not ashamed—people who did not have afflicted children.

The idea of a fund-raising campaign for Gateway needed some external validation. It was unlikely that this group would rally around a guy in baggy pants and Hawaiian shirts who was telling them to get over being ashamed of their children. The key would be getting Ken Plevin, Gateway's board chairman, to enthusiastically embrace the idea. I needed to recruit the type of expert Ken would listen to. My best friend, Larry, was one of New York's most successful professional fund-raisers, having masterminded huge campaigns for American Ballet Theatre, Public Television, and the NYU Medical Center. On top of that, the first five years of his career were spent raising money for a school for physically handicapped children. I knew I could count on Larry. He had always come through for me before, and he loved Joshua.

Ken was receptive to meeting with Larry, and a power breakfast at the legendary Carlyle Hotel was arranged. Davida Sherwood and Ellen joined the two men. I chose not to attend. Larry knew something about the alumni-parent base of potential supporters, and recognized many of the names of the parents of current Gateway students. He also knew the potential for fund-raising among my patients. Ken, a partner in one of New York's most prestigious law firms, asked many probing questions. In the end, Larry persuaded Ken and Davida that a devoted campaign committee might succeed, and offered to serve as a volunteer on the committee.

Larry returned from that meeting and told me how pessimistic everyone was. But as usual, Larry believed in me, and that made me feel better. Getting Larry on board was the first step, but I knew that I would need to establish more credibility.

A fortuitous circumstance occurred a few weeks later. Mark Kindgon, a well-known financier and philanthropist, and a patient of mine, called and wanted to donate some stock in the amount of about five thousand dollars. I called the school secretary to tell her to expect the call and was more amazed than upset at her response: She said she was very busy and asked me to call back in two weeks. Okay, I said to myself, this school is going to close and I call about a five thousand dollar donation and they tell me they are too busy. I considered getting angry for about ten seconds but then I realized that one of the reasons I loved Gateway was that the only thing that they ever worried about was the children. There was always time to do something for a child. Donations were another matter. I had to laugh. And I did.

Next, I decided to ask one of my patients for a donation. I had been taking care of Alex and Steve Cohen and their family for a long time. I knew that Steve made a nice living, and was hoping that Alex might help me with a donation. I was extremely embarrassed and felt like I was begging, but

I asked anyway. What happened next shocked me. While speaking with Alex after an appointment, I started to explain about Gateway and what I wanted but Alex just cut me off and said, "Here is a check for five thousand dollars." As I watched her write the check, shocked and overwhelmed by the amount and the generosity of her spirit, she asked, "How much do you really need." Half-joking I said, "Well, we could use a million dollars." To my amazement, she said, "Well, that is a lot of money. I will have to talk to Steve about it, but we'll see." Alex called me the next day and explained that she and Steve wanted to support Gateway, but they would do it over time. I thanked her profusely, and a few days later I received another check from her for fifteen thousand dollars. I called Ellen to tell her, and she took the check over to the school.

The fifteen thousand amazed and exhilarated everyone and I realized that there were people who wanted to help us but were just waiting for someone else to start. Then I got a call from Alex and she asked, "Hey, Dr. Roseman, what's going on? I gave you a check for fifteen thousand dollars and you lost it?" I had no idea what she was talking about, but it was pretty easy to find out. The school had lost the check and was embarrassed, so they blamed it on me. Alex's generosity of spirit once again surfaced and she said, "Don't worry, it happens all the time." Sure.

I had gotten the Gateway School two donations; the first they didn't have time for, and the other, they lost. But I had established some credibility as a fund-raiser for the school.

Word spread quickly about the Cohen donation, and people who had been hesitant to commit to the school were now ready. On Larry's suggestion, we started a school newsletter and announced the donations. I was shocked to find that now people were starting to believe that maybe we *could* save the school. Numerous people said to me, Well, if these guys are giving, perhaps we will, too.

Next I needed to shake up the schools' Board of Trustees. I needed someone dynamic who could change their attitude. I knew that it couldn't be me. I didn't look or sound the part, and the thought of sitting at a table for a meeting terrified me.

Denise Hurley, one of my patients, had all of the attributes that I lacked. She had gone to a seven sisters college and a top business school for her MBA, and she had an impressive business background. She spoke eloquently and with authority. I called on Ken Plevin. I needed Ken's assurance that he would help me get Denise on the board because I did not want to ask a patient to do this as a favor only to be humiliated by the board's rejection or equivocation. He said that if she would do it, he would take care of it.

I felt guilty about asking Denise to do this, and was very clear that I did not want her to feel obligated. Her answer must certainly stand out in the annals of charity and kindness as the epitome of the perfect potential board member of a charitable organization.

She said, "Okay, I know you need money and I will give, but how else can I help?"

I was hoping that her attitude would infect the rest of the board. I did not have to wait very long to find out.

A small party was planned so that we could ask people to help us raise money to save Gateway. It was to be held at the home of a high-profile alumni parent. However, just two weeks before the party, she told us that she would send in a sizable donation but could not have the party at her house. Denise, now a member of the Gateway Board, stepped in and offered to host the party. Denise and her husband, Al, a shining star at Merrill Lynch, had a spectacular apartment and a positive attitude about trying to help Gateway. Their attitude infected everyone at that party.

Over the next year Larry and I had to give pep talks to just about everybody at one time or another who felt depressed about the fate of the school. Even Ken. But then Ken did not need much of a pep talk; he was always ready to do whatever it took.

Afraid to scare people away, the board decided that our initial capital campaign was to be for $1.3 million. When we got close to that goal, the Board raised the goal to $3 million—still shy of the $5 million we needed, but people were now believers . . . or so I thought.

My wife, Ellen, shared her wealth of New York real estate development experience. She was instrumental in helping with the purchase of a building for $1.7 million and in overseeing renovations and expansion, which brought the cost up to exactly $5 million dollars. She was also on the capital campaign committee and the Board of Trustees, as well as other committees, and she was the VP of the parents association.

The parents' association seemed to have caught fire also. The school auction, which had originally been held in the school basement with people bringing tuna salad and home-baked cookies, was now being held at Sotheby's and raising hundreds of thousands of dollars. In a poignant moment before the start of the auction, the auctioneer spoke eloquently about his own problems and stated how happy and honored he was to be able to assist us.

At that point I thought that things were going great, but there was still tremendous trepidation when any of the parents who had done a lot for the school had to retire. The first major scare came when the children of the triumvirate of women who ran the auction graduated from Gateway. Once again I heard the musings about how we would never be able to replace them. There was a general feeling of panic. But other parents stepped up and the auction became better than ever, raising hundreds of thousands of dollars.

When it came time to start building, something happened that made me recognize something I had long repressed: No matter how much people like Joshua and me do, we will never receive the respect of others because we do not speak as well as, look as proper, or see things the same as other people. I was devastated, and it touched a nerve in me that I didn't realize existed.

I discovered this when a new board member was brought in, the grandmother of a recently admitted child. She hadn't been there during the darkest days when it seemed that Gateway would close its doors. She came in and saw that we had raised millions of dollars, had purchased a new building, and had hired architects and builders to start construction of the building. Suddenly she spoke up and said that she was worried that we would not be able to raise the rest of the money for the building. I couldn't blame her for her fears. But I was deeply hurt that the board panicked and halted the construction plans temporarily. I was shocked, angry, and distraught.

It was a devastating personal defeat. After years of my forging ahead and trying to impart my steel will on the rest of those involved, I was faced with the reality that few people had any faith in me. After years of guaranteeing that the school would be built, all it took for them to lose faith was a few words from the new kid's grandmother.

I went to speak to Dr. Sherwood about this. She had been at that first meeting when I stood up in my Hawaiian shirt and said that we could build a school. She had watched in amazement as things had progressed. Why, I asked, hadn't she spoken up for me? She knew I had promised her that somehow the school would be built; I wanted to know how, after all that had transpired, could she allow the words of one grandmother to convince her and the board that it might all be folly? I asked her if it was because I didn't look or sound the part. She said no, it had nothing to do with it, but

I knew that it did. The sadness in her eyes betrayed her true feelings.

I had been through a lifetime of people not believing in me because I was different. It used to make me angry. But I couldn't be angry with Dr. Sherwood; she had treated my son with enormous kindness, and for that I could forgive anything. In that moment I realized that my voyage was over. I had been delivered. I had overcome a lifetime of low self-esteem based on others' low expectations of me. I knew that because of Gateway my son would not have those feelings of worthlessness. As I stood to leave, I told her not to worry, that I would raise every cent myself if I had to. As it turned out, though, I didn't have to.

Things got back on track, but it was time for Ken Plevin to retire from the Board, and as the school cast about for a new chairman everyone felt trepidation about our next step.

One parent, a self-assured and successful banker, was the mother of a child with learning disabilities. When Larry and I met her, she was depressed, upset, and confused. She had seen this problem in family members and had blamed them, but now as she saw it in her own child she was grappling with the issue head-on for the first time. But there was something special about her. Although she was upset by her son's problems, she was not ashamed of her son, and as her son improved in Gateway, so did her mood and commitment to the school. She accepted the role of Chairman of the Board of Trustees and everyone breathed a sigh of relief.

It was now clear to everybody that no one person could

save a school. It had to be a joint effort by everyone involved. And the parents were responding in ways that were terrific. Not everyone could give money, but everyone wanted to help, and they did.

Suddenly, thanks to the effort of many parents and others who had taken up the cause of these children, Gateway received numerous prestigious grants from the Kresge Foundation, Starr Foundation, Educational Foundation of America, Hearst Foundation, and many others. It also received numerous personal donations and help from people who were touched by its mission.

The new Gateway School opened in September 2000, with a doubled enrollment of seventy children, almost none of whom have to pay for Gateway out of their own pockets. It is a breathtaking place with an unbelievable array of special features to help teach children with special needs. It has moved more than one parent to tears.

We need to raise more money to help pay for things for the kids, for outreach programs, and so on, but as always I have high hopes. I also have high hopes that other schools like this one will be built. Gateway has been offering advice freely for over thirty-five years to others who want to build schools or develop programs for children like my son Joshua, and will continue to do so.

My involvement with The Gateway School, once a source of shame for many, makes me swell with pride. I sense that many of the new parents feel the same way. The parents are doing amazing things to help their children and to reach out to others without shame, and that gratifies me.

I now find that, like my mother, I tell Joshua all the time that I hope that one day he will have a kid just like him because only then will he really understand what a glorious adventure it has been for me.

Select List of Resources for Adults and Children with ADD/ADHD, LD

The problem with listing resources is that there are so many available. I have tried to choose just a few good ones in each category.

E-MAIL

AKIDJUSTLIKEME@yahoo.com

AKIDJUSTLIKEME@netscape.com

AKIDJUSTLIKEME@hotmail.com

WEB SITES

www.akidjustlikeme.com

http://www.refdesk.com/health.html

http://www.nimh.nih.gov/publicat/adhd.cfm

http://mentalhelp.net/guide/adhd.htm

http://www.health-center.com/pharmacy/adhd/default.htm

http://www.Idonline.org/

http://www.ncld.org/

http://www.yahoo.com/Society and Culture/Disabilities/ Specific Disabilities/Learning Disabilities/

http://www.rit.edu/~easi/pubs/ldonelbw.htm

BOOKS

Hallowell, Edward M., and John J. Ratey. *Driven to Distraction: Recognizing and Coping with Attention Deficit Disorder from Childhood through Adulthood*, New York: Simon & Schuster, 1995.

Kelly, Kate. *You Mean I'm Not Lazy, Stupid or Crazy?!: A Self-Help Book for Adults with Attention Deficit Disorder*, New York: Simon & Schuster, 1995.

Kranowitz, Carol Stock. *The Out-Of-Sync Child: Recognizing and Coping with Sensory Integration Dysfunction*, New York: Perigee, 1998.

Mooney, Jonathan, and David Cole. *Learning Outside the Lines: Two Ivy League Students with Learning Disabilities and ADHD Give You the Tools for Academic Success and Educational Revolution*, New York: Simon & Schuster, 2000.

Robin, Arthur L. *ADHD in Adolescents: Diagnosis and Treatment*. New York: Guilford, 1999.

Silver, Larry B. *Attention-Deficit/Hyperactivity Disorder: A Clinical Guide to Diagnosis and Treatment for Health and*

Mental Health Professionals, New York: American Psychi-
atric Press, 1999.

Silver, Larry B. *Dr. Larry Silver's Advice to Parents on ADHD*.
New York: Crown Publishing Group, 1999.

Turecki, Stanley. *The Difficult Child*, New York: Bantam, 2000.

ORGANIZATIONS

CHADD: Children and Adults with Attention-Deficit/Hy-
peractivity Disorder
8181 Professional Place, Suite 201
Landover, MD 20785
Phone: 301/306-7070
Fax: 301/306-7090

HEATH Resource Center (Higher Education and Adult
Training for People with Disabilities)
One Dupont Circle, Suite 800
Washington, DC 20036
Phone: 202/939-9320 or 800/544-3284

Learning Disabilities Association of America
4156 Library Road
Pittsburgh, PA 15234
Telephone: 412/341-1515

Learning Disabilities Association of Canada
323 Chapel Street, #200
Ottawa, Ontario
K1N 7Z2 Canada
Telephone: 613/238-5721

National Center for Learning Disabilities
381 Park Ave. South, Suite 1401
New York, NY 10016
Telephone: 212/545-7510

National Institute for Child Health and Human Development
National Institutes of Health (NIH)
6100 Executive Boulevard
Rockville, MD 20852
Telephone: 301/496-5733

National Information Center for Children and Youth with Disabilities
P.O. Box 1492
Washington, DC 20013-1492
Telephone: 800/695-0285

National Association for Adults with Special Learning Needs
P.O. Box 716
Bryn Mawr, PA 19010
Telephone: 610/525-8336 or 800/869-8336

index

Page numbers in *italics* indicate figures; those in **bold** indicate tables.